THE BOOK OF COMMON PRAYER

Volume 1

SERVICES
and other material

CUM PRIVILEGIO

Giant Print Edition

CAMBRIDGE
UNIVERSITY PRESS

University Printing House, Cambridge CB2 8BS, United Kingdom

One Liberty Plaza, 20th Floor, New York, NY 10006, USA

477 Williamstown Road, Port Melbourne, VIC 3207, Australia

314-321, 3rd Floor, Plot 3, Splendor Forum, Jasola District Centre, New Delhi - 110025, India

79 Anson Road, #06-04/06, Singapore 079906

Cambridge University Press is part of the University of Cambridge.

It furthers the University's mission by disseminating knowledge in the pursuit of education, learning and research at the highest international levels of excellence.

www.cambridge.org
Information on this title: www.cambridge.org/9781108498616

Rights in the *Book of Common Prayer*
are vested in the Crown

This edition is published by
Cambridge University Press,
The Queen's Printer,
under Royal Letters Patent

First published 2005
This hardback edition 2019

Designed and typeset in 20/24pt Stone Sans (Adobe) by Peter Ducker MISTD
Published with support from Bealbury Methodist Chapel, St Mellion, Cornwall and
the Church Committee of The Mercers' Company, London

A catalogue record for this publication is available from the British Library

1. Services and other material   ISBN 978 1 108 49861 6
2. Collects, Epistles & Gospels   ISBN 978 1 108 49862 3
3. The Psalter   ISBN 978 0 521 61245 6

CONTENTS

iii

THE ORDER FOR
MORNING AND EVENING PRAYER

Daily to be said and used throughout the year

The Morning and Evening Prayer shall be used in the accustomed Place of the Church, Chapel, or Chancel; except it shall be otherwise determined by the Ordinary of the Place. And the Chancels shall remain as they have done in times past.

And here is to be noted, that such Ornaments of the Church, and of the Ministers thereof at all times of their Ministration, shall be retained, and be in use, as were in this Church of **England** by the Authority of Parliament, in the Second Year of the Reign of King **Edward** the Sixth.

Readers and such other lay persons as may be authorised by the Bishop of the diocese may, at the invitation of the Minister of the parish, or, where the Cure is vacant, or the Minister is incapacitated, at the invitation of the Churchwardens, say or sing Morning or Evening Prayer (save for the Absolution); and in case of need, where no clerk in Holy Orders or Reader or lay person authorised as aforesaid is available, the Minister or (failing him) the Churchwardens shall arrange for some suitable lay person to say or sing Morning or Evening Prayer (save for the Absolution).

THE ORDER FOR
MORNING PRAYER
DAILY THROUGHOUT
THE YEAR

At the beginning of Morning Prayer the Minister shall read with a loud voice some one or more of these Sentences of the Scriptures that follow. And then he shall say that which is written after the said Sentences.

WHEN the wicked man turneth away from his wickedness that he hath committed, and doeth that which is lawful and right, he shall save his soul alive.   *Ezek.* 18. 27.

I acknowledge my transgressions, and my sin is ever before me.   *Psalm* 51. 3.

Hide thy face from my sins, and blot out all mine iniquities.   *Psalm* 51. 9.

The sacrifices of God are a broken spirit : a broken and a contrite heart, O God, thou wilt not despise.   *Psalm* 51. 17.

Rend your heart, and not your garments, and turn unto the Lord your God: for he is gracious and merciful, slow to anger, and of great kindness, and repenteth him of the evil. *Joel* 2. 13.

To the Lord our God belong mercies and forgivenesses, though we have rebelled against him: neither have we obeyed the voice of the Lord our God, to walk in his laws which he set before us. *Dan.* 9. 9, 10.

O Lord, correct me, but with judgement; not in thine anger, lest thou bring me to nothing. *Jer.* 10. 24. *Psalm* 6. 1.

Repent ye; for the Kingdom of heaven is at hand. *S. Matth.* 3. 2.

I will arise and go to my father, and will say unto him, Father, I have sinned against heaven, and before thee, and am no more worthy to be called thy son. *S. Luke* 15. 18, 19.

Enter not into judgement with thy servant, O Lord; for in thy sight shall no man living be justified. *Psalm* 143. 2.

If we say that we have no sin, we deceive ourselves, and the truth is not in us: but if we confess our sins, he is faithful and just to forgive us our sins, and to cleanse us from all unrighteousness. 1 *S. John* 1. 8, 9.

DEARLY beloved brethren, the Scripture moveth us in sundry places to acknowledge and confess our manifold sins and wickedness; and that we should not dissemble nor cloke them before the face of Almighty God our heavenly Father; but confess them with an humble, lowly, penitent, and obedient heart; to the end that we may obtain forgiveness of the same, by his infinite goodness and mercy. And although we ought at all times humbly to acknowledge our sins before God; yet ought we most chiefly so to do, when we assemble and meet together to render thanks for the great benefits that we have received at his hands, to set forth his most worthy praise, to hear his most holy Word, and to ask those things which are requisite and necessary, as well for the body as the soul. Wherefore I pray and beseech you, as many as are here present, to accompany me with a pure heart and humble voice unto the throne of the heavenly grace, saying after me:

A general Confession to be said of the whole Congregation after the Minister, all kneeling.

ALMIGHTY and most merciful Father, We have erred and strayed from thy ways like lost sheep, We have followed too much the devices and desires of our own hearts, We have offended against thy holy laws, We have left undone those things which we ought to have done, And we have done those things which we ought not to have done, And there is no health in us: But thou, O Lord, have mercy upon us miserable offenders; Spare thou them, O God, which confess their faults, Restore thou them that are penitent, According to thy promises declared unto mankind in Christ Jesu our Lord: And grant, O most merciful Father, for his sake, That we may hereafter live a godly, righteous, and sober life, To the glory of thy holy Name. Amen.

The Absolution or Remission of sins to be pronounced by the Priest alone, standing: the people still kneeling.

ALMIGHTY God, the Father of our Lord Jesus Christ, who desireth not the death of a sinner, but rather that he may turn from his wickedness and live; and hath given power and commandment to his Ministers, to declare and pronounce to his people, being penitent, the Absolution and Remission of their sins: He pardoneth and absolveth all them that truly repent and unfeignedly believe his holy Gospel. Wherefore let us beseech him to grant us true repentance and his Holy Spirit, that those things may please him which we do at this present, and that the rest of our life hereafter may be pure and holy; so that at the last we may come to his eternal joy; through Jesus Christ our Lord.

The people shall answer here, and at the end of all other prayers,

Amen.

If no priest be present the person saying the Service shall read the Collect for the Twenty-First Sunday after Trinity, that person and the people still kneeling.

Then the Minister shall kneel, and say the Lord's Prayer with an audible voice: the people also kneeling, and repeating it with him, both here, and wheresoever else it is used in Divine Service.

OUR Father which art in heaven, Hallowed be thy Name, Thy kingdom come, Thy will be done, in earth as it is in heaven. Give us this day our daily bread; And forgive us our trespasses, As we forgive them that trespass against us; And lead us not into temptation, But deliver us from evil. For thine is the kingdom, the power, and the glory, For ever and ever. Amen.

Then likewise he shall say,

O Lord, open thou our lips.

Answer. And our mouth shall shew forth thy praise.

Priest. O God, make speed to save us.

Answer. O Lord, make haste to help us.

Here, all standing up, the Priest shall say,

Glory be to the Father, and to the Son: and to the Holy Ghost;

Answer. As it was in the beginning, is now and ever shall be: world without end. Amen.

Priest. Praise ye the Lord.

Answer. The Lord's Name be praised.

Then shall be said or sung this Psalm following: Except on Easter Day, upon which another Anthem is appointed: and on the nineteenth day of every month it is not to be read here, but in the ordinary course of the Psalms.

VENITE, EXULTEMUS DOMINO

PSALM 95

O COME, let us sing unto the Lord : let us heartily rejoice in the strength of our salvation.

Let us come before his presence with thanksgiving : and shew ourselves glad in him with psalms.

For the Lord is a great God : and a great King above all gods.

In his hand are all the corners of the earth : and the strength of the hills is his also.

The sea is his, and he made it : and his hands prepared the dry land.

O come, let us worship, and fall down : and kneel before the Lord our Maker.

For he is the Lord our God : and we are the people of his pasture, and the sheep of his hand.

To day if ye will hear his voice, harden not your hearts : as in the provocation, and as in the day of temptation in the wilderness;

When your fathers tempted me : proved me, and saw my works.

Forty years long was I grieved with this generation, and said : It is a people that do err in their hearts, for they have not known my ways.

Unto whom I sware in my wrath : that they should not enter into my rest.

Glory be to the Father, and to the Son : and to the Holy Ghost;

As it was in the beginning, is now, and ever shall be : world without end. Amen.

Then shall follow the Psalms in order as they be appointed. And at the end of every Psalm throughout the year, and likewise in the end of Benedicite, Benedictus, Magnificat, and Nunc dimittis, shall be repeated,

Glory be to the Father, and to the Son: and to the Holy Ghost;

Answer. As it was in the beginning, is now, and ever shall be: world without end. Amen.

Then shall be read distinctly with an audible voice the First Lesson, taken out of the Old Testament as is appointed in the Calendar: Except there be proper Lessons assigned for that day: He that readeth so standing and turning himself, as he may best be heard of all such as are present. And after that shall be said or sung, in English, the Hymn called Te Deum Laudamus, daily throughout the year.

Note that before every Lesson the Minister shall say, **Here beginneth such a Chapter**, or **Verse of such a Chapter, of such a Book**: And after every Lesson, **Here endeth the First**, or **the Second Lesson.**

TE DEUM LAUDAMUS

WE praise thee, O God : we acknowledge thee to be the Lord.

All the earth doth worship thee : the Father everlasting.

To thee all Angels cry aloud : the heavens and all the powers therein.

To thee Cherubin and Seraphin : continually do cry,

Holy, Holy, Holy : Lord God of Sabaoth;

Heaven and earth are full of the Majesty : of thy glory.

The glorious company of the Apostles : praise thee.

The goodly fellowship of the Prophets : praise thee.

The noble army of Martyrs : praise thee.

The holy Church throughout all the world : doth acknowledge thee;

The Father : of an infinite Majesty;

Thine honourable, true : and only Son;

Also the Holy Ghost : the Comforter.

Thou art the King of glory : O Christ.

Thou art the everlasting Son : of the Father.

When thou tookest upon thee to deliver man : thou didst not abhor the Virgin's womb.

When thou hadst overcome the sharpness of

death : thou didst open the kingdom of heaven to all believers.

Thou sittest at the right hand of God : in the glory of the Father.

We believe that thou shalt come : to be our Judge.

We therefore pray thee, help thy servants : whom thou hast redeemed with thy precious blood.

Make them to be numbered with thy Saints : in glory everlasting.

O Lord, save thy people : and bless thine heritage.

Govern them : and lift them up for ever.

Day by day : we magnify thee;

And we worship thy Name : ever world without end.

Vouchsafe, O Lord : to keep us this day without sin.

O Lord, have mercy upon us : have mercy upon us.

O Lord, let thy mercy lighten upon us : as our trust is in thee.

O Lord, in thee have I trusted : let me never be confounded.

Or this Canticle,

BENEDICITE, OMNIA OPERA

O ALL ye Works of the Lord, bless ye the Lord : praise him, and magnify him for ever.

O ye Angels of the Lord, bless ye the Lord : praise him, and magnify him for ever.

O ye Heavens, bless ye the Lord : praise him, and magnify him for ever.

O ye Waters that be above the Firmament, bless ye the Lord : praise him, and magnify him for ever.

O all ye Powers of the Lord, bless ye the Lord : praise him, and magnify him for ever.

O ye Sun and Moon, bless ye the Lord : praise him, and magnify him for ever.

O ye Stars of Heaven, bless ye the Lord : praise him, and magnify him for ever.

O ye Showers and Dew, bless ye the Lord : praise him, and magnify him for ever.

O ye Winds of God, bless ye the Lord : praise him, and magnify him for ever.

O ye Fire and Heat, bless ye the Lord : praise him, and magnify him for ever.

O ye Winter and Summer, bless ye the Lord : praise him, and magnify him for ever.

O ye Dews and Frosts, bless ye the Lord : praise him, and magnify him for ever.

O ye Frost and Cold, bless ye the Lord : praise him, and magnify him for ever.

O ye Ice and Snow, bless ye the Lord : praise him, and magnify him for ever.

O ye Nights and Days, bless ye the Lord : praise him, and magnify him for ever.

O ye Light and Darkness, bless ye the Lord : praise him, and magnify him for ever.

O ye Lightnings and Clouds, bless ye the Lord : praise him, and magnify him for ever.

O let the Earth bless the Lord : yea, let it praise him, and magnify him for ever.

O ye Mountains and Hills, bless ye the Lord : praise him, and magnify him for ever.

O all ye Green Things upon the Earth, bless

ye the Lord : praise him, and magnify him for ever.

O ye Wells, bless ye the Lord : praise him, and magnify him for ever.

O ye Seas and Floods, bless ye the Lord : praise him, and magnify him for ever.

O ye Whales, and all that move in the Waters, bless ye the Lord : praise him, and magnify him for ever.

O all ye Fowls of the Air, bless ye the Lord : praise him, and magnify him for ever.

O all ye Beasts and Cattle, bless ye the Lord : praise him, and magnify him for ever.

O ye Children of Men, bless ye the Lord : praise him, and magnify him for ever.

O let Israel bless the Lord : praise him, and magnify him for ever.

O ye Priests of the Lord, bless ye the Lord : praise him, and magnify him for ever.

O ye Servants of the Lord, bless ye the Lord : praise him, and magnify him for ever.

O ye Spirits and Souls of the Righteous, bless

ye the Lord : praise him, and magnify him for ever.

O ye holy and humble Men of heart, bless ye the Lord : praise him, and magnify him for ever.

O Ananias, Azarias, and Misael, bless ye the Lord : praise him, and magnify him for ever.

Glory be to the Father, and to the Son : and to the Holy Ghost;

As it was in the beginning, is now, and ever shall be : world without end. Amen.

Then shall be read in like manner the Second Lesson, taken out of the New Testament. And after that the Hymn following: Except when that shall happen to be read in the Chapter for the day, or for the Gospel on Saint John Baptist's Day.

BENEDICTUS

S. LUKE 1. 68

BLESSED be the Lord God of Israel : for he hath visited, and redeemed his people;

And hath raised up a mighty salvation for us : in the house of his servant David;

As he spake by the mouth of his holy

Prophets : which have been since the world began;

That we should be saved from our enemies : and from the hands of all that hate us;

To perform the mercy promised to our fore-fathers : and to remember his holy covenant;

To perform the oath which he sware to our forefather Abraham : that he would give us;

That we being delivered out of the hands of our enemies : might serve him without fear;

In holiness and righteousness before him : all the days of our life.

And thou, child, shalt be called the Prophet of the Highest : for thou shalt go before the face of the Lord to prepare his ways;

To give knowledge of salvation unto his people : for the remission of their sins;

Through the tender mercy of our God : whereby the day-spring from on high hath visited us;

To give light to them that sit in darkness, and in the shadow of death : and to guide our feet into the way of peace.

Glory be to the Father, and to the Son : and to the Holy Ghost;

As it was in the beginning, is now, and ever shall be : world without end. Amen.

Or this Psalm,

JUBILATE DEO

PSALM 100

O BE joyful in the Lord, all ye lands : serve the Lord with gladness, and come before his presence with a song.

Be ye sure that the Lord he is God : it is he that hath made us, and not we ourselves; we are his people, and the sheep of his pasture.

O go your way into his gates with thanksgiving, and into his courts with praise : be thankful unto him, and speak good of his Name.

For the Lord is gracious, his mercy is everlasting : and his truth endureth from generation to generation.

Glory be to the Father, and to the Son : and to the Holy Ghost;

As it was in the beginning, is now, and ever shall be : world without end. Amen.

Then shall be sung or said the Apostles' Creed, by the Minister and the people standing: Except only such days as the Creed of Saint Athanasius is appointed to be read.

I BELIEVE in God the Father Almighty, Maker of heaven and earth:

And in Jesus Christ his only Son our Lord, Who was conceived by the Holy Ghost, Born of the Virgin Mary, Suffered under Pontius Pilate, Was crucified, dead, and buried: He descended into hell; The third day he rose again from the dead; He ascended into heaven, And sitteth on the right hand of God the Father Almighty; From thence he shall come to judge the quick and the dead.

I believe in the Holy Ghost; The holy Catholick Church; The Communion of Saints; The Forgiveness of sins; The Resurrection of the body, And the life everlasting. Amen.

And after that these Prayers following, all devoutly kneeling: the Minister first pronouncing with a loud voice,

The Lord be with you.
Answer. And with thy spirit.
Minister. Let us pray.
Lord, have mercy upon us.
Christ, have mercy upon us.
Lord, have mercy upon us.

Then the Minister, Clerks, and people shall say the Lord's Prayer with a loud voice.

OUR Father which art in heaven, Hallowed be thy Name, Thy kingdom come, Thy will be done, in earth as it is in heaven. Give us this day our daily bread; And forgive us our trespasses, As we forgive them that trespass against us; And lead us not into temptation, But deliver us from evil. Amen.

Then the Priest standing up shall say,
O Lord, shew thy mercy upon us.
Answer. And grant us thy salvation.
Priest. O Lord, save the Queen.
Answer. And mercifully hear us when we call upon thee.

Priest. Endue thy Ministers with righteousness.

Answer. And make thy chosen people joyful.

Priest. O Lord, save thy people.

Answer. And bless thine inheritance.

Priest. Give peace in our time, O Lord.

Answer. Because there is none other that fighteth for us, but only thou, O God.

Priest. O God, make clean our hearts within us.

Answer. And take not thy Holy Spirit from us.

Then shall follow three Collects: The first of the day, which shall be the same that is appointed at the Communion: The second for Peace: The third for Grace to live well. And the two last Collects shall never alter, but daily be said at Morning Prayer throughout all the year, as followeth, all kneeling.

THE SECOND COLLECT, FOR PEACE.

O GOD, who art the author of peace and lover of concord, in knowledge of whom standeth our eternal life, whose service is perfect freedom: Defend us thy humble servants in all assaults of our enemies; that we, surely trusting in thy defence, may not fear the power of any adversaries; through the might of Jesus Christ our Lord. **Amen.**

THE THIRD COLLECT, FOR GRACE.

O LORD our heavenly Father, Almighty and everlasting God, who hast safely brought us to the beginning of this day: Defend us in the same with thy mighty power; and grant that this day we fall into no sin, neither run into any kind of danger; but that all our doings may be ordered by thy governance, to do always that is righteous in thy sight; through Jesus Christ our Lord. **Amen.**

In Quires and Places where they sing here followeth the Anthem.

Then these five Prayers following are to be read here: Except when the Litany is read; and then only the two last are to be read, as they are there placed.

A PRAYER FOR THE QUEEN'S MAJESTY.

O LORD our heavenly Father, high and mighty, King of kings, Lord of lords, the only Ruler of princes, who dost from thy throne behold all the dwellers upon earth: Most heartily we beseech thee with thy favour to behold our most gracious Sovereign Lady, Queen **ELIZABETH**; and so replenish her with the grace of thy Holy Spirit, that she may alway incline to thy will, and walk in thy way: Endue her plenteously with heavenly gifts; grant her in health and wealth long to live; strengthen her that she may vanquish and overcome all her enemies, and finally after this life she may attain everlasting joy and felicity; through Jesus Christ our Lord. **Amen.**

A PRAYER FOR THE ROYAL FAMILY.

ALMIGHTY God, the fountain of all goodness, we humbly beseech thee to bless **Philip** Duke of Edinburgh, **Charles** Prince of Wales, and all the Royal Family; Endue them with thy Holy Spirit; enrich them with thy heavenly grace; prosper them with all happiness; and bring them to thine everlasting kingdom; through Jesus Christ our Lord. **Amen.**

A PRAYER FOR THE CLERGY AND PEOPLE.

ALMIGHTY and everlasting God, who alone workest great marvels: Send down upon our Bishops and Curates, and all Congregations committed to their charge, the healthful Spirit of thy grace; and that they may truly please thee, pour upon them the continual dew of thy blessing. Grant this, O Lord, for the honour of our Advocate and Mediator, Jesus Christ. **Amen.**

A PRAYER OF SAINT CHRYSOSTOM.

ALMIGHTY God, who hast given us grace at this time with one accord to make our common supplications unto thee; and dost promise that when two or three are gathered together in thy Name thou wilt grant their requests: Fulfil now, O Lord, the desires and petitions of thy servants, as may be most expedient for them; granting us in this world knowledge of thy truth, and in the world to come life everlasting. **Amen.**

2 CORINTHIANS 13.

THE grace of our Lord Jesus Christ, and the love of God, and the fellowship of the Holy Ghost, be with us all evermore. **Amen.**

**Here endeth the Order of Morning Prayer
throughout the Year.**

THE ORDER FOR
EVENING PRAYER
DAILY THROUGHOUT
THE YEAR

At the beginning of Evening Prayer the Minister shall read with a loud voice some one or more of these Sentences of the Scriptures that follow. And then he shall say that which is written after the said Sentences.

WHEN the wicked man turneth away from his wickedness that he hath committed, and doeth that which is lawful and right, he shall save his soul alive. *Ezek.* 18. 27.

I acknowledge my transgressions, and my sin is ever before me. *Psalm* 51. 3.

Hide thy face from my sins, and blot out all mine iniquities. *Psalm* 51. 9.

The sacrifices of God are a broken spirit : a broken and a contrite heart, O God, thou wilt not despise. *Psalm* 51. 17.

Rend your heart, and not your garments, and turn unto the Lord your God: for he is gracious and merciful, slow to anger, and of great kindness, and repenteth him of the evil.

Joel 2. 13.

To the Lord our God belong mercies and forgivenesses, though we have rebelled against him: neither have we obeyed the voice of the Lord our God, to walk in his laws which he set before us. *Dan.* 9. 9, 10.

O Lord, correct me, but with judgement; not in thine anger, lest thou bring me to nothing.

Jer. 10. 24. *Psalm* 6. 1.

Repent ye; for the Kingdom of heaven is at hand. *S. Matth.* 3. 2.

I will arise and go to my father, and will say unto him, Father, I have sinned against heaven, and before thee, and am no more worthy to be called thy son. *S. Luke* 15. 18, 19.

Enter not into judgement with thy servant, O Lord; for in thy sight shall no man living be justified. *Psalm* 143. 2.

If we say that we have no sin, we deceive ourselves, and the truth is not in us: but if we confess our sins, he is faithful and just to forgive us our sins, and to cleanse us from all unrighteousness. *1 S. John* 1. 8, 9.

DEARLY beloved brethren, the Scripture moveth us in sundry places to acknowledge and confess our manifold sins and wickedness; and that we should not dissemble nor cloke them before the face of Almighty God our heavenly Father; but confess them with an humble, lowly, penitent, and obedient heart; to the end that we may obtain forgiveness of the same, by his infinite goodness and mercy. And although we ought at all times humbly to acknowledge our sins before God; yet ought we most chiefly so to do, when we assemble and meet together to render thanks for the great benefits that we have received at his hands, to set forth his most worthy praise, to hear his most holy Word, and to ask those things which are requisite and necessary, as well for the body as the soul. Wherefore I pray and beseech you, as many as are here present, to accompany me with a pure heart and humble voice unto the throne of the heavenly grace, saying after me:

A general Confession to be said of the whole Congregation after the Minister, all kneeling.

ALMIGHTY and most merciful Father, We have erred and strayed from thy ways like lost sheep, We have followed too much the devices and desires of our own hearts, We have offended against thy holy laws, We have left undone those things which we ought to have done, And we have done those things which we ought not to have done, And there is no health in us: But thou, O Lord, have mercy upon us miserable offenders; Spare thou them, O God, which confess their faults, Restore thou them that are penitent, According to thy promises declared unto mankind in Christ Jesu our Lord: And grant, O most merciful Father, for his sake, That we may hereafter live a godly, righteous, and sober life, To the glory of thy holy Name. Amen.

The Absolution or Remission of sins to be pronounced by the Priest alone, standing: the people still kneeling.

ALMIGHTY God, the Father of our Lord Jesus Christ, who desireth not the death of a sinner, but rather that he may turn from his wickedness and live; and hath given power and commandment to his Ministers, to declare and pronounce to his people, being penitent, the Absolution and Remission of their sins: He pardoneth and absolveth all them that truly repent and unfeignedly believe his holy Gospel. Wherefore let us beseech him to grant us true repentance and his Holy Spirit, that those things may please him which we do at this present, and that the rest of our life hereafter may be pure and holy; so that at the last we may come to his eternal joy; through Jesus Christ our Lord. **Amen.**

If no priest be present the person saying the Service shall read the Collect for the Twenty-First Sunday after Trinity, that person and the people still kneeling.

Then the Minister shall kneel, and say the Lord's Prayer: the people also kneeling, and repeating it with him.

OUR Father which art in heaven, Hallowed be thy Name, Thy kingdom come, Thy will be done, in earth as it is in heaven. Give us this day our daily bread; And forgive us our trespasses, As we forgive them that trespass against us; And lead us not into temptation, But deliver us from evil. For thine is the kingdom, the power, and the glory, For ever and ever. Amen.

Then likewise he shall say,

O Lord, open thou our lips.

Answer. And our mouth shall shew forth thy praise.

Priest. O God, make speed to save us.

Answer. O Lord, make haste to help us.

Here, all standing up, the Priest shall say,

Glory be to the Father, and to the Son: and to the Holy Ghost;

Answer. As it was in the beginning, is now, and ever shall be: world without end. Amen.

Priest. Praise ye the Lord.

Answer. The Lord's Name be praised.

Then shall be said or sung the Psalms in order as they be appointed. Then a Lesson of the Old Testament, as is appointed. And after that Magnificat (or the Song of the Blessed Virgin Mary) in English, as followeth.

MAGNIFICAT

S. LUKE 1

MY soul doth magnify the Lord : and my spirit hath rejoiced in God my Saviour.

For he hath regarded : the lowliness of his hand-maiden.

For behold, from henceforth : all generations shall call me blessed.

For he that is mighty hath magnified me : and holy is his Name.

And his mercy is on them that fear him : throughout all generations.

He hath shewed strength with his arm : he hath scattered the proud in the imagination of their hearts.

He hath put down the mighty from their seat : and hath exalted the humble and meek.

He hath filled the hungry with good things : and the rich he hath sent empty away.

He remembering his mercy hath holpen his servant Israel : as he promised to our fore-fathers, Abraham and his seed for ever.

Glory be to the Father, and to the Son : and to the Holy Ghost;

As it was in the beginning, is now, and ever shall be : world without end. Amen.

Or else this Psalm: Except it be on the nineteenth day of the month, when it is read in the ordinary course of the Psalms.

CANTATE DOMINO

PSALM 98

O SING unto the Lord a new song : for he hath done marvellous things.

With his own right hand, and with his holy arm : hath he gotten himself the victory.

The Lord declared his salvation : his right-eousness hath he openly shewed in the sight of the heathen.

He hath remembered his mercy and truth toward the house of Israel : and all the ends of the world have seen the salvation of our God.

Shew yourselves joyful unto the Lord, all ye lands : sing, rejoice, and give thanks.

Praise the Lord upon the harp : sing to the harp with a psalm of thanksgiving.

With trumpets also and shawms : O shew yourselves joyful before the Lord the King.

Let the sea make a noise, and all that therein is : the round world, and they that dwell therein.

Let the floods clap their hands, and let the hills be joyful together before the Lord : for he cometh to judge the earth.

With righteousness shall he judge the world : and the people with equity.

Glory be to the Father, and to the Son : and to the Holy Ghost;

As it was in the beginning, is now, and ever shall be : world without end. Amen.

Then a Lesson of the New Testament, as it is appointed. And after that Nunc dimittis (or the Song of Simeon) in English, as followeth.

NUNC DIMITTIS

S. LUKE 2. 29

LORD, now lettest thou thy servant depart in peace: according to thy word.

For mine eyes have seen : thy salvation;

Which thou hast prepared : before the face of all people;

To be a light to lighten the Gentiles : and to be the glory of thy people Israel.

Glory be to the Father, and to the Son : and to the Holy Ghost;

As it was in the beginning, is now, and ever shall be : world without end. Amen.

Or else this Psalm: Except it be on the twelfth day of the month.

DEUS MISEREATUR

PSALM 67

GOD be merciful unto us, and bless us : and shew us the light of his countenance, and be merciful unto us:

That thy way may be known upon earth : thy saving health among all nations.

Let the people praise thee, O God : yea, let all the people praise thee.

O let the nations rejoice and be glad : for thou shalt judge the folk righteously, and govern the nations upon earth.

Let the people praise thee, O God : yea, let all the people praise thee.

Then shall the earth bring forth her increase : and God, even our own God, shall give us his blessing.

God shall bless us : and all the ends of the world shall fear him.

Glory be to the Father, and to the Son : and to the Holy Ghost;

As it was in the beginning, is now, and ever shall be : world without end. Amen.

Then shall be said or sung the Apostles' Creed, by the Minister and the people standing.

I BELIEVE in God the Father Almighty, Maker of heaven and earth:

And in Jesus Christ his only Son our Lord, Who was conceived by the Holy Ghost, Born of the Virgin Mary, Suffered under Pontius Pilate, Was crucified, dead, and buried: He descended into hell; The third day he rose again from the dead; He ascended into heaven, And sitteth on the right hand of God the Father Almighty; From thence he shall come to judge the quick and the dead.

I believe in the Holy Ghost; The holy Catholick Church; The Communion of Saints; The Forgiveness of sins; The Resurrection of the body, And the life everlasting. Amen.

And after that these Prayers following, all devoutly kneeling: the Minister first pronouncing with a loud voice,

The Lord be with you.
Answer. And with thy spirit.
   Minister. Let us pray.
Lord, have mercy upon us.
   Christ, have mercy upon us.
Lord, have mercy upon us.

Then the Minister, Clerks, and people shall say the Lord's Prayer with a loud voice.

OUR Father which art in heaven, Hallowed be thy Name, Thy kingdom come, Thy will be done, in earth as it is in heaven. Give us this day our daily bread; And forgive us our trespasses, As we forgive them that trespass against us; And lead us not into temptation, But deliver us from evil. Amen.

Then the Priest standing up shall say,

O Lord, shew thy mercy upon us.

Answer. And grant us thy salvation.

Priest. O Lord, save the Queen.

Answer. And mercifully hear us when we call upon thee.

Priest. Endue thy Ministers with righteousness.

Answer. And make thy chosen people joyful.

Priest. O Lord, save thy people.

Answer. And bless thine inheritance.

Priest. Give peace in our time, O Lord.

Answer. Because there is none other that fighteth for us, but only thou, O God.

Priest. O God, make clean our hearts within us.

Answer. And take not thy Holy Spirit from us.

Then shall follow three Collects: The first of the day: The second for Peace: The third for Aid against all Perils, as hereafter followeth: which two last Collects shall be daily said at Evening Prayer without alteration.

THE SECOND COLLECT AT EVENING PRAYER.

O GOD, from whom all holy desires, all good counsels, and all just works do proceed: Give unto thy servants that peace which the world cannot give; that both our hearts may be set to obey thy commandments, and also that by thee we being defended from the fear of our enemies may pass our time in rest and quietness; through the merits of Jesus Christ our Saviour. **Amen.**

THE THIRD COLLECT, FOR AID AGAINST ALL PERILS.

LIGHTEN our darkness, we beseech thee, O Lord; and by thy great mercy defend us from all perils and dangers of this night; for the love of thy only Son, our Saviour Jesus Christ. **Amen.**

In Quires and Places where they sing here followeth the Anthem.

A PRAYER FOR THE QUEEN'S MAJESTY.

O LORD our heavenly Father, high and mighty, King of kings, Lord of lords, the only Ruler of princes, who dost from thy throne behold all the dwellers upon earth: Most heartily we beseech thee with thy favour to behold our most gracious Sovereign Lady, Queen **ELIZABETH**; and so replenish her with the grace of thy Holy Spirit, that she may alway incline to thy will, and walk in thy way: Endue her plenteously with heavenly gifts; grant her in health and wealth long to live; strengthen her that she may vanquish and overcome all her enemies, and finally after this life she may attain everlasting joy and felicity; through Jesus Christ our Lord. **Amen.**

A PRAYER FOR THE ROYAL FAMILY.

ALMIGHTY God, the fountain of all goodness, we humbly beseech thee to bless **Philip** Duke of Edinburgh, **Charles** Prince of Wales, and all the Royal Family: Endue them with thy Holy Spirit; enrich them with thy heavenly grace; prosper them with all happiness; and bring them to thine everlasting kingdom; through Jesus Christ our Lord. **Amen.**

A PRAYER FOR THE CLERGY AND PEOPLE.

ALMIGHTY and everlasting God, who alone workest great marvels: Send down upon our Bishops and Curates, and all Congregations committed to their charge, the healthful Spirit of thy grace; and that they may truly please thee, pour upon them the continual dew of thy blessing. Grant this, O Lord, for the honour of our Advocate and Mediator, Jesus Christ. **Amen.**

A PRAYER OF SAINT CHRYSOSTOM.

ALMIGHTY God, who hast given us grace at this time with one accord to make our common supplications unto thee; and dost promise that when two or three are gathered together in thy Name thou wilt grant their requests: Fulfil now, O Lord, the desires and petitions of thy servants, as may be most expedient for them; granting us in this world knowledge of thy truth, and in the world to come life everlasting. **Amen.**

2 CORINTHIANS 13.

THE grace of our Lord Jesus Christ, and the love of God, and the fellowship of the Holy Ghost, be with us all evermore. **Amen.**

Here endeth the Order of Evening Prayer throughout the Year.

AT
MORNING PRAYER

Upon these Feasts; **Christmas Day**, the **Epiphany**, **Saint Matthias**, **Easter Day**, **Ascension Day**, **Whitsunday**, Saint **John Baptist**, Saint **James**, Saint **Bartholomew**, Saint **Matthew**, Saint **Simon** and Saint **Jude**, Saint **Andrew**, and upon **Trinity Sunday**, shall be sung or said at Morning Prayer, instead of the Apostles' Creed, this Confession of our Christian Faith, commonly called the Creed of Saint Athanasius, by the Minister and people standing.

QUICUNQUE VULT

WHOSOEVER will be saved : before all things it is necessary that he hold the Catholick Faith.

Which Faith except every one do keep whole and undefiled : without doubt he shall perish everlastingly.

And the Catholick Faith is this : That we worship one God in Trinity, and Trinity in Unity;

Neither confounding the Persons: nor dividing the Substance.

For there is one Person of the Father, another of the Son : and another of the Holy Ghost.

But the Godhead of the Father, of the Son, and of the Holy Ghost, is all one : the Glory equal, the Majesty co-eternal.

Such as the Father is, such is the Son : and such is the Holy Ghost.

The Father uncreate, the Son uncreate : and the Holy Ghost uncreate.

The Father incomprehensible, the Son incomprehensible : and the Holy Ghost incomprehensible.

The Father eternal, the Son eternal : and the Holy Ghost eternal.

And yet they are not three eternals : but one eternal.

As also there are not three incomprehensibles, nor three uncreated : but one uncreated, and one incomprehensible.

So likewise the Father is Almighty, the Son Almighty : and the Holy Ghost Almighty.

And yet they are not three Almighties : but one Almighty.

So the Father is God, the Son is God : and the Holy Ghost is God.

And yet they are not three Gods : but one God.

So likewise the Father is Lord, the Son Lord : and the Holy Ghost Lord.

And yet not three Lords : but one Lord.

For like as we are compelled by the Christian verity : to acknowledge every Person by himself to be God and Lord;

So are we forbidden by the Catholick Religion : to say there be three Gods, or three Lords.

The Father is made of none : neither created, nor begotten.

The Son is of the Father alone : not made, nor created, but begotten.

The Holy Ghost is of the Father and of the Son : neither made, nor created, nor begotten, but proceeding.

So there is one Father, not three Fathers; one Son, not three Sons : one Holy Ghost, not three Holy Ghosts.

And in this Trinity none is afore, or after other : none is greater, or less than another;

But the whole three Persons are co-eternal together : and co-equal.

So that in all things, as is aforesaid : the Unity in Trinity, and the Trinity in Unity is to be worshipped.

He therefore that will be saved : must thus think of the Trinity.

Furthermore it is necessary to everlasting salvation : that he also believe rightly the Incarnation of our Lord Jesus Christ.

For the right Faith is that we believe and confess : that our Lord Jesus Christ, the Son of God, is God and Man;

God, of the Substance of the Father, begotten before the worlds : and Man, of the Substance of his Mother, born in the world;

Perfect God, and Perfect Man : of a reasonable soul and human flesh subsisting;

Equal to the Father, as touching his Godhead : and inferior to the Father, as touching his Manhood.

Who although he be God and Man : yet he is not two, but one Christ;

One, not by conversion of the Godhead into flesh : but by taking of the Manhood into God;

One altogether, not by confusion of Substance : but by unity of Person.

For as the reasonable soul and flesh is one man : so God and Man is one Christ.

Who suffered for our salvation : descended into hell, rose again the third day from the dead.

He ascended into heaven, he sitteth on the right hand of the Father, God Almighty : from whence he shall come to judge the quick and the dead.

At whose coming all men shall rise again with their bodies : and shall give account for their own works.

And they that have done good shall go into life everlasting : and they that have done evil into everlasting fire.

This is the Catholick Faith : which except a man believe faithfully, he cannot be saved.

Glory be to the Father, and to the Son : and to the Holy Ghost;

As it was in the beginning, is now, and ever shall be : world without end. Amen.

THE LITANY

Here followeth the Litany, or General Supplication, to be sung or said after Morning Prayer, upon Sundays, Wednesdays, and Fridays, and at other times when it shall be commanded by the Ordinary.

O GOD the Father of heaven : have mercy upon us miserable sinners.

O God the Father of heaven : have mercy upon us miserable sinners.

O God the Son, Redeemer of the world : have mercy upon us miserable sinners.

O God the Son, Redeemer of the world : have mercy upon us miserable sinners.

O God the Holy Ghost, proceeding from the Father and the Son : have mercy upon us miserable sinners.

O God the Holy Ghost, proceeding from the Father and the Son : have mercy upon us miserable sinners.

O holy, blessed, and glorious Trinity, three Persons and one God : have mercy upon us miserable sinners.

O holy, blessed, and glorious Trinity, three Persons and one God : have mercy upon us miserable sinners.

Remember not, Lord, our offences, nor the offences of our forefathers; neither take thou vengeance of our sins : spare us, good Lord, spare thy people, whom thou hast redeemed with thy most precious blood, and be not angry with us for ever.

Spare us, good Lord.

From all evil and mischief; from sin, from the crafts and assaults of the devil; from thy wrath, and from everlasting damnation,

Good Lord, deliver us.

From all blindness of heart; from pride, vain-glory, and hypocrisy; from envy, hatred, and malice, and all uncharitableness,

Good Lord, deliver us.

From fornication, and all other deadly sin;

and from all the deceits of the world, the flesh, and the devil,

Good Lord, deliver us.

From lightning and tempest; from plague, pestilence, and famine; from battle and murder, and from sudden death,

Good Lord, deliver us.

From all sedition, privy conspiracy, and rebellion; from all false doctrine, heresy, and schism; from hardness of heart, and contempt of thy Word and Commandment,

Good Lord, deliver us.

By the mystery of thy holy Incarnation; by thy holy Nativity and Circumcision; by thy Baptism, Fasting, and Temptation,

Good Lord, deliver us.

By thine Agony and bloody Sweat; by thy Cross and Passion; by thy precious Death and Burial; by thy glorious Resurrection and Ascension; and by the coming of the Holy Ghost,

Good Lord, deliver us.

In all time of our tribulation; in all time of our

wealth; in the hour of death, and in the day of judgement,

Good Lord, deliver us.

We sinners do beseech thee to hear us, O Lord God : and that it may please thee to rule and govern thy holy Church universal in the right way,

We beseech thee to hear us, good Lord.

That it may please thee to keep and strengthen in the true worshipping of thee, in righteousness and holiness of life, thy Servant **ELIZABETH**, our most gracious Queen and Governor,

We beseech thee to hear us, good Lord.

That it may please thee to rule her heart in thy faith, fear, and love, and that she may evermore have affiance in thee, and ever seek thy honour and glory,

We beseech thee to hear us, good Lord.

That it may please thee to be her defender and keeper, giving her the victory over all her enemies,

We beseech thee to hear us, good Lord.

That it may please thee to bless and preserve **Philip** Duke of Edinburgh, **Charles** Prince of Wales, and all the Royal Family,

We beseech thee to hear us, good Lord.

That it may please thee to illuminate all Bishops, Priests, and Deacons, with true knowledge and understanding of thy Word; and that both by their preaching and living they may set it forth and shew it accordingly,

We beseech thee to hear us, good Lord.

That it may please thee to endue the Lords of the Council, and all the Nobility, with grace, wisdom, and understanding,

We beseech thee to hear us, good Lord.

That it may please thee to bless and keep the Magistrates, giving them grace to execute justice, and to maintain truth,

We beseech thee to hear us, good Lord.

That it may please thee to bless and keep all thy people,

We beseech thee to hear us, good Lord.

That it may please thee to give to all nations unity, peace, and concord,

We beseech thee to hear us, good Lord.

That it may please thee to give us an heart to love and dread thee, and diligently to live after thy commandments,

We beseech thee to hear us, good Lord.

That it may please thee to give to all thy people increase of grace, to hear meekly thy Word, and to receive it with pure affection, and to bring forth the fruits of the Spirit,

We beseech thee to hear us, good Lord.

That it may please thee to bring into the way of truth all such as have erred, and are deceived,

We beseech thee to hear us, good Lord.

That it may please thee to strengthen such as do stand; and to comfort and help the weak-hearted; and to raise up them that fall; and finally to beat down Satan under our feet,

We beseech thee to hear us, good Lord.

That it may please thee to succour, help, and comfort all that are in danger, necessity, and tribulation,

We beseech thee to hear us, good Lord.

That it may please thee to preserve all that travel by land or by water, all women labouring of child, all sick persons, and young children; and to shew thy pity upon all prisoners and captives,

We beseech thee to hear us, good Lord.

That it may please thee to defend, and provide for, the father-less children, and widows, and all that are desolate and oppressed,

We beseech thee to hear us, good Lord.

That it may please thee to have mercy upon all men,

We beseech thee to hear us, good Lord.

That it may please thee to forgive our enemies, persecutors, and slanderers, and to turn their hearts,

We beseech thee to hear us, good Lord.

That it may please thee to give and preserve to our use the kindly fruits of the earth, so as in due time we may enjoy them,

We beseech thee to hear us, good Lord.

That it may please thee to give us true repentance; to forgive us all our sins, negligences, and ignorances; and to endue us with the grace of thy Holy Spirit, to amend our lives according to thy holy Word,

We beseech thee to hear us, good Lord.

Son of God: we beseech thee to hear us.

Son of God: we beseech thee to hear us.

O Lamb of God: that takest away the sins of the world;

Grant us thy peace.

O Lamb of God: that takest away the sins of the world;

Have mercy upon us.

O Christ, hear us.

O Christ, hear us.

Lord, have mercy upon us.

Lord, have mercy upon us.

Christ, have mercy upon us.

Christ, have mercy upon us.

Lord, have mercy upon us.

Lord, have mercy upon us.

Then shall the Priest, and the people with him, say the Lord's Prayer.

OUR Father which art in heaven, Hallowed be thy Name, Thy kingdom come, Thy will be done, in earth as it is in heaven. Give us this day our daily bread; And forgive us our trespasses, As we forgive them that trespass against us; And lead us not into temptation, But deliver us from evil. Amen.

Priest. O Lord, deal not with us after our sins.

Answer. Neither reward us after our iniquities.

Let us pray.

O GOD, merciful Father, that despisest not the sighing of a contrite heart, nor the desire of such as be sorrowful: Mercifully assist our prayers that we make before thee in all our troubles and adversities, whensoever they oppress us; and graciously hear us, that those evils, which the craft and subtilty of the devil or man worketh against us, be brought to nought, and by the providence of thy goodness they may be dispersed; that we thy servants, being hurt by no persecutions, may evermore give thanks unto thee in thy holy Church; through Jesus Christ our Lord.

O Lord, arise, help us, and deliver us for thy Name's sake.

O GOD, we have heard with our ears, and our fathers have declared unto us, the noble works that thou didst in their days, and in the old time before them.

O Lord, arise, help us, and deliver us for thine honour.

Glory be to the Father, and to the Son: and to the Holy Ghost;
Answer. As it was in the beginning, is now, and ever shall be : world without end. Amen.

From our enemies defend us, O Christ.
Graciously look upon our afflictions.
Pitifully behold the sorrows of our hearts.
Mercifully forgive the sins of thy people.
Favourably with mercy hear our prayers.
O Son of David, have mercy upon us.

Both now and ever vouchsafe to hear us, O Christ.

Graciously hear us, O Christ; graciously hear us, O Lord Christ.

Priest. O Lord, let thy mercy be shewed upon us;

Answer. As we do put our trust in thee.

Let us pray.

WE humbly beseech thee, O Father, mercifully to look upon our infirmities; and for the glory of thy Name turn from us all those evils that we most righteously have deserved; and grant that in all our troubles we may put our whole trust and confidence in thy mercy, and evermore serve thee in holiness and pureness of living, to thy honour and glory; through our only Mediator and Advocate, Jesus Christ our Lord. **Amen.**

A PRAYER OF SAINT CHRYSOSTOM.

ALMIGHTY God, who hast given us grace at this time with one accord to make our common supplications unto thee; and dost promise that when two or three are gathered together in thy Name thou wilt grant their requests: Fulfil now, O Lord, the desires and petitions of thy servants, as may be most expedient for them; granting us in this world knowledge of thy truth, and in the world to come life everlasting. **Amen.**

2 CORINTHIANS 13.

THE grace of our Lord Jesus Christ, and the love of God, and the fellowship of the Holy Ghost, be with us all evermore. **Amen.**

Here endeth the Litany.

PRAYERS AND THANKSGIVINGS

Upon several occasions, to be used before the two final Prayers of the Litany, or of Morning and Evening Prayer.

PRAYERS

For Rain.

O GOD, heavenly Father, who by thy Son Jesus Christ hast promised to all them that seek thy kingdom, and the righteousness thereof, all things necessary to their bodily sustenance: Send us, we beseech thee, in this our necessity, such moderate rain and showers, that we may receive the fruits of the earth to our comfort, and to thy honour; through Jesus Christ our Lord. **Amen.**

For fair Weather.

O ALMIGHTY Lord God, who for the sin of man didst once drown all the world, except eight persons, and afterward of thy great mercy didst promise never to destroy it so again: We humbly beseech thee, that although we for our iniquities have worthily deserved a plague of rain and waters, yet upon our true repentance thou wilt send us such weather, as that we may receive the fruits of the earth in due season; and learn both by thy punishment to amend our lives, and for thy clemency to give thee praise and glory; through Jesus Christ our Lord. **Amen.**

In the time of Dearth and Famine.

O GOD, heavenly Father, whose gift it is that the rain doth fall, the earth is fruitful, beasts increase, and fishes do multiply: Behold, we beseech thee, the afflictions of thy people; and grant that the scarcity and dearth, which we do now most justly suffer for our iniquity, may through thy goodness be mercifully turned into cheapness and plenty; for the love of Jesus Christ our Lord, to whom with thee and the Holy Ghost be all honour and glory, now and for ever. **Amen.**

Or this.

O GOD, merciful Father, who, in the time of Elisha the prophet, didst suddenly in Samaria turn great scarcity and dearth into plenty and cheapness: Have mercy upon us, that we, who are now for our sins punished with like adversity, may likewise find a seasonable relief: Increase the fruits of the earth by thy heavenly benediction; and grant that we, receiving thy bountiful liberality, may use the same to thy glory, the relief of those that are needy, and our own comfort; through Jesus Christ our Lord. **Amen.**

In the time of War and Tumults.

O ALMIGHTY God, King of all kings, and Governor of all things, whose power no creature is able to resist, to whom it belongeth justly to punish sinners, and to be merciful to them that truly repent: Save and deliver us, we humbly beseech thee, from the hands of our enemies; abate their pride, asswage their malice, and confound their devices; that we, being armed with thy defence, may be preserved evermore from all perils, to glorify thee, who art the only giver of all victory; through the merits of thy only Son, Jesus Christ our Lord. **Amen.**

In the time of any common Plague or Sickness.

O ALMIGHTY God, who in thy wrath didst send a plague upon thine own people in the wilderness, for their obstinate rebellion against Moses and Aaron; and also, in the time of king David, didst slay with the plague of pestilence threescore and ten thousand, and yet remembering thy mercy didst save the rest: Have pity upon us miserable sinners, who now are visited with great sickness and mortality; that like as thou didst then accept of an atonement, and didst command the destroying Angel to cease from punishing, so it may now please thee to withdraw from us this plague and grievous sickness; through Jesus Christ our Lord. **Amen.**

In the Ember Weeks, to be said every day, for those that are to be admitted into Holy Orders.

ALMIGHTY God, our heavenly Father, who hast purchased to thyself an universal Church by the precious blood of thy dear Son: Mercifully look upon the same, and at this time so guide and govern the minds of thy servants the Bishops and Pastors of thy flock, that they may lay hands suddenly on no man, but faithfully and wisely make choice of fit persons to serve in the sacred Ministry of thy Church. And to those which shall be ordained to any holy function give thy grace and heavenly benediction; that both by their life and doctrine they may set forth thy glory, and set forward the salvation of all men; through Jesus Christ our Lord. **Amen.**

Or this.

ALMIGHTY God, the giver of all good gifts, who of thy divine providence hast appointed divers Orders in thy Church: Give thy grace, we humbly beseech thee, to all those who are to be called to any office and administration in the same; and so replenish them with the truth of thy doctrine, and endue them with innocency of life, that they may faithfully serve before thee, to the glory of thy great Name, and the benefit of thy holy Church; through Jesus Christ our Lord. **Amen.**

A Prayer that may be said after any of the former.

O GOD, whose nature and property is ever to have mercy and to forgive, receive our humble petitions; and though we be tied and bound with the chain of our sins, yet let the pitifulness of thy great mercy loose us; for the honour of Jesus Christ, our Mediator and Advocate. **Amen.**

A Prayer for the High Court of Parliament, to be read during their Session.

MOST gracious God, we humbly beseech thee, as for this Kingdom in general, so especially for the High Court of Parliament, under our most religious and gracious Queen at this time assembled: That thou wouldest be pleased to direct and prosper all their consultations to the advancement of thy glory, the good of thy Church, the safety, honour, and welfare of our Sovereign and her Dominions; that all things may be so ordered and settled by their endeavours, upon the best and surest foundations, that peace and happiness, truth and justice, religion and piety, may be established among us for all generations. These and all other necessaries, for them, for us, and thy whole Church, we humbly beg in the Name and Mediation of Jesus Christ our most blessed Lord and Saviour. **Amen.**

A Collect or Prayer for all Conditions of men, to be used at such times when the Litany is not appointed to be said.

O GOD, the Creator and Preserver of all mankind, we humbly beseech thee for all sorts and conditions of men; that thou wouldest be pleased to make thy ways known unto them, thy saving health unto all nations. More especially we pray for the good estate of the Catholick Church; that it may be so guided and governed by thy good Spirit, that all who profess and call themselves Christians may be led into the way of truth, and hold the faith in unity of spirit, in the bond of peace, and in righteousness of life. Finally we commend to thy fatherly goodness all those, who are any ways afflicted or distressed in mind, body, or estate; [*especially those for whom our prayers are desired;] that it may please thee to comfort and relieve them, according to their several necessities, giving them patience under their sufferings, and a happy issue out of all their afflictions. And this we beg for Jesus Christ his sake. Amen.

[*This to be said when any desire the Prayers of the Congregation.]

THANKSGIVINGS

A General Thanksgiving.

ALMIGHTY God, Father of all mercies, we thine unworthy servants do give thee most humble and hearty thanks for all thy goodness and loving-kindness to us and to all men; [‡particularly to those who desire now to offer up their praises and thanksgivings for thy late mercies vouchsafed unto them.] We bless

[‡This to be said when any that have been prayed for desire to return praise.]

thee for our creation, preservation, and all the blessings of this life; but above all for thine inestimable love in the redemption of the world by our Lord Jesus Christ, for the means of grace, and for the hope of glory. And we beseech thee, give us that due sense of all thy mercies, that our hearts may be unfeignedly thankful, and that we shew forth thy praise, not only with our lips, but in our lives; by giving up ourselves to thy service, and by walking before thee in holiness and righteousness all our days; through Jesus Christ our Lord, to whom with thee and the Holy Ghost be all honour and glory, world without end. **Amen.**

For Rain.

O GOD our heavenly Father, who by thy gracious providence dost cause the former and the latter rain to descend upon the earth, that it may bring forth fruit for the use of man: We give thee humble thanks that it hath pleased thee, in our great necessity, to send us at the last a joyful rain upon thine inheritance, and to refresh it when it was dry, to the great comfort of us thy unworthy servants, and to the glory of thy holy Name; through thy mercies in Jesus Christ our Lord. **Amen.**

For fair Weather.

O LORD God, who hast justly humbled us by thy late plague of immoderate rain and waters, and in thy mercy hast relieved and comforted our souls by this seasonable and blessed change of weather: We praise and glorify thy holy Name for this thy mercy, and will always declare thy loving-kindness from generation to generation; through Jesus Christ our Lord. **Amen.**

For Plenty.

O MOST merciful Father, who of thy gracious goodness hast heard the devout prayers of thy Church, and turned our dearth and scarcity into cheapness and plenty: We give thee humble thanks for this thy special bounty; beseeching thee to continue thy loving-kindness unto us, that our land may yield us her fruits of increase, to thy glory and our comfort; through Jesus Christ our Lord. **Amen.**

For Peace and Deliverance from our Enemies.

O ALMIGHTY God, who art a strong tower of defence unto thy servants against the face of their enemies: We yield thee praise and thanksgiving for our deliverance from those great and apparent dangers wherewith we were compassed: We acknowledge it thy goodness that we were not delivered over as a prey unto them; beseeching thee still to continue such thy mercies towards us, that all the world may know that thou art our Saviour and mighty Deliverer; through Jesus Christ our Lord. **Amen.**

For restoring Publick Peace at Home.

O ETERNAL God, our heavenly Father, who alone makest men to be of one mind in a house, and stillest the outrage of a violent and unruly people: We bless thy holy Name, that it hath pleased thee to appease the seditious tumults which have been lately raised up amongst us: most humbly beseeching thee to grant to all of us grace, that we may henceforth obediently walk in thy holy commandments; and leading a quiet and peaceable life, in all godliness and honesty, may continually offer unto thee our sacrifice of praise and thanksgiving for these thy mercies towards us; through Jesus Christ our Lord. **Amen.**

For Deliverance from the Plague, or other common Sickness.

O LORD God, who hast wounded us for our sins, and consumed us for our transgressions, by thy late heavy and dreadful visitation; and now, in the midst of judgement remembering mercy, hast redeemed our souls from the jaws of death: We offer unto thy fatherly goodness ourselves, our souls and bodies which thou hast delivered, to be a living sacrifice unto thee, always praising and magnifying thy mercies in the midst of thy Church; through Jesus Christ our Lord. **Amen.**

Or this.

WE humbly acknowledge before thee, O most merciful Father, that all the punishments which are threatened in thy law might justly have fallen upon us, by reason of our manifold transgressions and hardness of heart: Yet seeing it hath pleased thee of thy tender mercy, upon our weak and unworthy humiliation, to asswage the contagious sickness wherewith we lately have been sore afflicted, and to restore the voice of joy and health into our dwellings: We offer unto thy Divine Majesty the sacrifice of praise and thanksgiving, lauding and magnifying thy glorious Name for such thy preservation and providence over us; through Jesus Christ our Lord. **Amen.**

THE ORDER
FOR THE ADMINISTRATION
OF
THE LORD'S SUPPER
OR
HOLY COMMUNION

So many as intend to be partakers of the holy Communion shall signify their names to the Curate, at least some time the day before.

If a Minister be persuaded that any person who presents himself to be a partaker of the holy Communion ought not to be admitted thereunto by reason of malicious and open contention with his neighbours, or other grave and open sin without repentance, he shall give an account of the same to the Ordinary of the place, and therein obey his order and direction, but so as not to refuse the Sacrament to any person until in accordance with such order and direction he shall have called him and advertised him that in any wise he presume not to come to the Lord's Table; Provided that in case of grave and immediate scandal to the Congregation the Minister shall not admit such person, but shall give an account of the same to the Ordinary within seven days after at the latest and therein obey the order and direction given to him by the Ordinary; Provided also that before issuing his order and direction in relation to any such person the Ordinary shall afford to him an opportunity for interview.

The Table at the Communion time having a fair white linen cloth upon it, shall stand in the body of the Church, or in the Chancel, where Morning and Evening Prayer are appointed to be said. And the Priest standing at the north side of the Table shall say the Lord's Prayer with the Collect following, the people kneeling.

OUR Father which art in heaven, Hallowed be thy Name, Thy kingdom come, Thy will be done, in earth as it is in heaven. Give us this day our daily bread; And forgive us our trespasses, As we forgive them that trespass against us; And lead us not into temptation, But deliver us from evil. Amen.

THE COLLECT

ALMIGHTY God, unto whom all hearts be open, all desires known, and from whom no secrets are hid: Cleanse the thoughts of our hearts by the inspiration of thy Holy Spirit, that we may perfectly love thee, and worthily magnify thy holy Name; through Christ our Lord. **Amen.**

Then shall the Priest, turning to the people, rehearse distinctly all the TEN COMMANDMENTS: and the people still kneeling shall after every Commandment ask God mercy for their transgression thereof for the time past, and grace to keep the same for the time to come, as followeth.

Minister.

GOD spake these words, and said; I am the Lord thy God: Thou shalt have none other gods but me.

People. Lord, have mercy upon us, and incline our hearts to keep this law.

Minister. Thou shalt not make to thyself any graven image, nor the likeness of any thing that is in heaven above, or in the earth beneath, or in the water under the earth. Thou shalt not bow down to them, nor worship them. For I the Lord thy God am a jealous God, and visit the sins of the fathers upon the children unto the third and fourth generation of them that hate me, and shew mercy unto thousands in them that love me and keep my commandments.

People. Lord, have mercy upon us, and incline our hearts to keep this law.

Minister. Thou shalt not take the Name of the Lord thy God in vain: for the Lord will not hold him guiltless, that taketh his Name in vain.

People. Lord, have mercy upon us, and incline our hearts to keep this law.

Minister. Remember that thou keep holy the Sabbath day. Six days shalt thou labour, and do all that thou hast to do; but the seventh day is the Sabbath of the Lord thy God. In it thou shalt do no manner of work, thou, and thy son, and thy daughter, thy man-servant, and thy maid-servant, thy cattle, and the stranger that is within thy gates. For in six days the Lord made heaven and earth, the sea, and all that in them is, and rested the seventh day: wherefore the Lord blessed the seventh day, and hallowed it.

People. Lord, have mercy upon us, and incline our hearts to keep this law.

Minister. Honour thy father and thy mother; that thy days may be long in the land which the Lord thy God giveth thee.

People. Lord, have mercy upon us, and incline our hearts to keep this law.

Minister. Thou shalt do no murder.

People. Lord, have mercy upon us, and incline our hearts to keep this law.

Minister. Thou shalt not commit adultery.

People. Lord, have mercy upon us, and incline our hearts to keep this law.

Minister. Thou shalt not steal.

People. Lord, have mercy upon us, and incline our hearts to keep this law.

Minister. Thou shalt not bear false witness against thy neighbour.

People. Lord, have mercy upon us, and incline our hearts to keep this law.

Minister. Thou shalt not covet thy neighbour's house, thou shalt not covet thy neighbour's wife, nor his servant, nor his maid, nor his ox, nor his ass, nor any thing that is his.

People. Lord, have mercy upon us, and write all these thy laws in our hearts, we beseech thee.

Then shall follow one of these two Collects for the Queen, the Priest standing as before, and saying,

Let us pray.

ALMIGHTY God, whose kingdom is ever lasting, and power infinite: Have mercy upon the whole Church; and so rule the heart of thy chosen servant **ELIZABETH**, our Queen and Governor, that she (knowing whose minister she is) may above all things seek thy honour and glory: and that we and all her subjects (duly considering whose authority she hath) may faithfully serve, honour, and humbly obey her, in thee, and for thee, according to thy blessed Word and ordinance; through Jesus Christ our Lord, who with thee and the Holy Ghost liveth and reigneth, ever one God, world without end. **Amen.**

Or,

ALMIGHTY and everlasting God, we are taught by thy holy Word, that the hearts of Kings are in thy rule and governance, and that thou dost dispose and turn them as it seemeth best to thy godly wisdom: We humbly beseech thee so to dispose and govern the heart of **ELIZABETH** thy servant, our Queen and Governor, that in all her thoughts, words, and works, she may ever seek thy honour and glory, and study to preserve thy people committed to her charge, in wealth, peace and godliness: Grant this, O merciful Father, for thy dear Son's sake, Jesus Christ our Lord. **Amen.**

Then shall be said the Collect of the Day. And immediately after the Collect the Priest shall read the Epistle, saying, The Epistle [or, The portion of Scripture appointed for the Epistle] is written in the —— Chapter of —— beginning at the —— Verse. And the Epistle ended, he shall say, Here endeth the Epistle. Then shall he read the Gospel (the people all standing up) saying, The holy Gospel is written in the —— Chapter of —— beginning at the —— Verse. And the Gospel ended, shall be sung or said the Creed following, the people still standing as before.

I BELIEVE in one God the Father Almighty, Maker of heaven and earth, And of all things visible and invisible:

And in one Lord Jesus Christ, the only-begotten Son of God, Begotten of his Father before all worlds, God of God, Light of Light, Very God of very God, Begotten, not made, Being of one substance with the Father, By whom all things were made: Who for us men and for our salvation came down from heaven, And was incarnate by the Holy Ghost of the Virgin Mary, And was made man, And was crucified also for us under Pontius Pilate. He suffered and was buried, And the third day he rose again according to the Scriptures, And ascended into heaven, And sitteth on the right hand of the Father. And he shall come again with glory to judge both the quick and the dead: Whose kingdom shall have no end.

And I believe in the Holy Ghost, The Lord and giver of life, Who proceedeth from the Father and the Son, Who with the Father and the Son together is worshipped and glorified, Who spake by the Prophets. And I believe one Catholick and Apostolick Church. I acknowledge one Baptism for the remission of sins. And I look for the Resurrection of the dead, And the life of the world to come. Amen.

Then the Curate shall declare unto the people what Holy-days, or Fasting-days, are in the week following to be observed. And then also (if occasion be) shall notice be given of the Communion; and Briefs, Citations, and Excommunications read. And nothing shall be proclaimed or published in the Church during the time of Divine Service, but by the Minister: nor by him any thing but what is prescribed in the Rules of this Book, or enjoined by the Queen, or by the Ordinary of the place.

Then shall follow the Sermon, or one of the Homilies already set forth, or hereafter to be set forth, by authority.

Then shall the Priest return to the Lord's Table, and begin the Offertory, saying one or more of these Sentences following, as he thinketh most convenient in his discretion.

LET your light so shine before men, that they may see your good works, and glorify your Father which is in heaven. *S. Matth.* 5.

Lay not up for yourselves treasure upon the earth; where the rust and moth doth corrupt, and where thieves break through and steal: but lay up for yourselves treasures in heaven; where neither rust nor moth doth corrupt, and where thieves do not break through and steal. *S. Matth.* 6.

Whatsoever ye would that men should do unto you, even so do unto them; for this is the Law and the Prophets.   *S. Matth.* 7.

Not every one that saith unto me, Lord, Lord, shall enter into the kingdom of heaven; but he that doeth the will of my Father which is in heaven.   *S. Matth.* 7.

Zacchæus stood forth, and said unto the Lord, Behold, Lord, the half of my goods I give to the poor; and if I have done any wrong to any man, I restore four-fold.   *S. Luke* 19.

Who goeth a warfare at any time of his own cost? who planteth a vineyard, and eateth not of the fruit thereof? or who feedeth a flock, and eateth not of the milk of the flock?
                                        1 *Cor.* 9.

If we have sown unto you spiritual things, is it a great matter if we shall reap your worldly things?   1 *Cor.* 9.

Do ye not know that they who minister about holy things live of the sacrifice; and they who wait at the altar are partakers with the altar? Even so hath the Lord also ordained, that they who preach the Gospel should live of the Gospel. *1 Cor. 9.*

He that soweth little shall reap little; and he that soweth plenteously shall reap plenteously. Let every man do according as he is disposed in his heart, not grudging, or of necessity; for God loveth a cheerful giver. *2 Cor. 9.*

Let him that is taught in the word minister unto him that teacheth, in all good things. Be not deceived, God is not mocked: for whatsoever a man soweth that shall he reap. *Gal. 6.*

While we have time, let us do good unto all men; and specially unto them that are of the household of faith. *Gal. 6.*

Godliness is great riches, if a man be content with that he hath: for we brought nothing into the world, neither may we carry any thing out. *1 Tim. 6.*

Charge them who are rich in this world, that they be ready to give, and glad to distribute; laying up in store for themselves a good foundation against the time to come, that they may attain eternal life. *1 Tim. 6.*

God is not unrighteous, that he will forget your works, and labour that proceedeth of love; which love ye have shewed for his name's sake, who have ministered unto the saints, and yet do minister. *Hebr.* 6.

To do good and to distribute forget not; for with such sacrifices God is pleased. *Hebr.* 13.

Whoso hath this world's good, and seeth his brother have need, and shutteth up his compassion from him, how dwelleth the love of God in him? 1 *S. John* 3.

Give alms of thy goods, and never turn thy face from any poor man; and then the face of the Lord shall not be turned away from thee.
Tobit 4.

Be merciful after thy power. If thou hast much, give plenteously; if thou hast little, do thy diligence gladly to give of that little; for so gatherest thou thyself a good reward in the day of necessity. *Tobit* 4.

He that hath pity upon the poor lendeth unto the Lord: and look, what he layeth out, it shall be paid him again. *Prov.* 19.

Blessed be the man that provideth for the sick and needy: the Lord shall deliver him in the time of trouble. *Psal.* 41.

Whilst these Sentences are in reading, the Deacons, Churchwardens, or other fit person appointed for that purpose, shall receive the Alms for the Poor, and other devotions of the people, in a decent bason to be provided by the Parish for that purpose; and reverently bring it to the Priest, who shall humbly present and place it upon the holy Table.

And when there is a Communion, the Priest shall then place upon the Table so much Bread and Wine as he shall think sufficient. After which done, the Priest shall say,

Let us pray for the whole state of Christ's Church militant here in earth.

ALMIGHTY and everliving God, who by thy holy Apostle hast taught us to make prayers and supplications, and to give thanks, for all men: We humbly beseech thee most mercifully [***to accept our alms and oblations, and**] to receive these our prayers, which we offer unto

*If there be no alms or oblations, then shall the words [**of accepting our alms and oblations**] be left out unsaid.

thy Divine Majesty; beseeching thee to inspire continually the universal Church with the spirit of truth, unity, and concord: And grant, that all they that do confess thy holy Name may agree in the truth of thy holy Word, and live in unity, and godly love. We beseech thee also to save and defend all Christian Kings, Princes, and Governors; and specially thy servant **ELIZABETH** our Queen; that under her we may be godly and quietly governed: And grant unto her whole Council, and to all that are put in authority under her, that they may truly and indifferently minister justice, to the punishment of wickedness and vice, and to the maintenance of thy true religion, and virtue. Give grace, O heavenly Father, to all Bishops and Curates, that they may both by their life and doctrine set forth thy true and lively Word, and rightly and duly administer thy holy Sacraments: And to all thy people give thy heavenly grace; and specially to this congregation here present; that, with meek heart and due reverence, they may hear, and receive thy holy Word; truly serving thee in holiness and righteousness all the days of their life. And we most humbly beseech thee of thy goodness, O Lord, to comfort and succour all them, who in this transitory life are in trouble, sorrow, need, sickness, or any other adversity. And we also bless thy holy Name for all thy servants departed this life in thy faith and fear; beseeching thee to give us grace so to follow their good examples, that with them we may be partakers of thy heavenly kingdom: Grant this, O Father, for Jesus Christ's sake, our only Mediator and Advocate. **Amen.**

When the Minister giveth warning for the Celebration of the holy Communion, (which he shall always do upon the Sunday, or some Holy-day, immediately preceding,) after the Sermon or Homily ended, he shall read this Exhortation following.

DEARLY beloved, on ——day next I purpose, through God's assistance, to administer to all such as shall be religiously and devoutly disposed the most comfortable Sacrament of the Body and Blood of Christ; to be by them received in remembrance of his meritorious Cross and Passion, whereby alone we obtain remission of our sins, and are made partakers of the kingdom of heaven. Wherefore it is our duty to render most humble and hearty thanks to Almighty God our heavenly Father, for that he hath given his Son our Saviour Jesus Christ, not only to die for us, but also to be our spiritual food and sustenance in that holy Sacrament. Which being so divine and comfortable a thing to them who receive it worthily, and so dangerous to them that will presume to receive it unworthily; my duty is to exhort you in the mean season to consider the dignity of that holy mystery, and the great peril of the unworthy receiving thereof; and so to search and examine your own consciences, and that not lightly, and after the manner of dissemblers with God: but so that ye may come holy and clean to such a heavenly Feast, in the marriage-garment required by God in holy Scripture, and be received as worthy partakers of that holy Table.

The way and means thereto is; First, to examine your lives and conversations by the rule of God's commandments; and whereinsoever ye shall perceive yourselves to have offended, either by will, word, or deed, there to bewail your own sinfulness, and to confess yourselves to Almighty God, with full purpose of amendment of life. And if ye shall perceive your offences to be such as are not only against God, but also against your neighbours; then ye shall reconcile yourselves unto them; being ready to make restitution and satisfaction, according to the uttermost of your powers, for all injuries and wrongs done by you to any other; and being likewise ready to forgive others that have offended you, as you would have forgiveness of your offences at God's hand; for otherwise the receiving of the holy Communion doth nothing else but increase your damnation. Therefore if any of you be a blasphemer of God, an hinderer or slanderer of his Word, an adulterer, or be in malice, or envy, or in any other grievous crime, repent you of your sins, or else come not to that holy Table; lest, after the taking of that holy Sacrament, the devil enter into you, as he entered into Judas, and fill you full of all iniquities, and bring you to destruction both of body and soul.

And because it is requisite, that no man should come to the holy Communion, but with a full trust in God's mercy, and with a quiet conscience; therefore if there be any of you, who by this means cannot quiet his own conscience herein, but requireth further comfort or counsel, let him come to me, or to some other discreet and learned Minister of God's Word, and open his grief; that by the ministry of God's holy Word he may receive the benefit of absolution, together with ghostly counsel and advice, to the quieting of his conscience, and avoiding of all scruple and doubtfulness.

Or, in case he shall see the people negligent to come to the holy Communion, instead of the former, he shall use this Exhortation.

DEARLY beloved brethren, on —— I intend, by

God's grace, to celebrate the Lord's Supper: unto which, in God's behalf, I bid you all that are here present; and beseech you, for the Lord Jesus Christ's sake, that ye will not refuse to come thereto, being so lovingly called and bidden by God himself. Ye know how grievous and unkind a thing it is, when a man hath prepared a rich feast, decked his table with all kind of provision, so that there lacketh nothing but the guests to sit down; and yet they who are called (without any cause) most unthankfully refuse to come. Which of you in such a case would not be moved? Who would not think a great injury and wrong done unto him? Wherefore, most dearly beloved in Christ, take ye good heed, lest ye, withdrawing yourselves from this holy Supper, provoke God's indignation against you. It is an easy matter for a man to say, I will not communicate, because I am otherwise hindered with worldly business. But such excuses are not so easily accepted and allowed before God. If any man say, I am a grievous sinner, and therefore am afraid to come: wherefore then do ye not repent and amend? When God calleth you, are ye not ashamed to say ye will not come? When ye should return to God, will ye excuse yourselves, and say ye are not ready? Consider earnestly with yourselves how little such feigned excuses will avail before God. They that refused the feast in the Gospel, because they had bought a farm, or would try their yokes of oxen, or because they were married, were not so excused, but counted unworthy of the heavenly feast. I, for my part, shall be ready; and, according to mine Office, I bid you in the Name of God, I call you in Christ's behalf, I exhort you, as ye love your own salvation, that ye will be partakers of this holy Communion. And as the Son of God did vouchsafe to yield up his soul by death upon the Cross for your salvation; so it is your duty to receive the Communion, in remembrance of the sacrifice of his death, as he himself hath commanded: which if ye shall neglect to do, consider with yourselves how great injury ye do unto God, and how sore punishment hangeth over your heads for the same; when ye wilfully abstain from the Lord's Table, and separate from your brethren, who come to feed on the banquet of that most heavenly food. These things if ye earnestly consider, ye will by God's grace return to a better mind: for the obtaining whereof we shall not cease to make our humble petitions unto Almighty God our heavenly Father.

At the time of the Celebration of the Communion, the Communicants being conveniently placed for the receiving of the holy Sacrament, the Priest shall say this Exhortation.

DEARLY beloved in the Lord, ye that mind to come to the holy Communion of the Body and Blood of our Saviour Christ, must consider how Saint Paul exhorteth all persons diligently to try and examine themselves, before they presume to eat of that Bread, and drink of that Cup. For as the benefit is great, if with a true penitent heart and lively faith we receive that holy Sacrament; (for then we spiritually eat the flesh of Christ, and drink his blood; then we dwell in Christ, and Christ in us; we are one with Christ, and Christ with us;) so is the danger great, if we receive the same unworthily. For then we are guilty of the Body and Blood of Christ our Saviour; we eat and drink our own damnation, not considering the Lord's Body; we kindle God's wrath against us; we provoke him to plague us with divers diseases, and sundry kinds of death. Judge therefore yourselves, brethren, that ye be not judged of the Lord; repent you truly for your sins past; have a lively and stedfast faith in Christ our Saviour; amend your lives, and be in perfect charity with all men; so shall ye be meet partakers of those holy mysteries. And above all things ye must give most humble and hearty thanks to God, the Father, the Son, and the Holy Ghost, for the redemption of the world by the death and passion of our Saviour Christ, both God and man; who did humble himself, even to the death upon the Cross, for us miserable sinners, who lay in darkness and the shadow of death; that he might make us the children of God, and exalt us to everlasting life. And to the end that we should alway remember the exceeding great love of our Master and only Saviour Jesus Christ, thus dying for us, and the innumerable benefits which by his precious blood-shedding he hath obtained to us; he hath instituted and ordained holy mysteries, as pledges of his love, and for a continual remembrance of his death, to our great and endless comfort. To him therefore, with the Father and the Holy Ghost, let us give (as we are most bounden) continual thanks; submitting ourselves wholly to his holy will and pleasure, and studying to serve him in true holiness and righteousness all the days of our life. **Amen.**

Then shall the Priest say to them that come to receive the holy Communion,

YE that do truly and earnestly repent you of your sins, and are in love and charity with your neighbours, and intend to lead a new life, following the commandments of God, and walking from henceforth in his holy ways:

Draw near with faith, and take this holy Sacrament to your comfort; and make your humble confession to Almighty God, meekly kneeling upon your knees.

Then shall this general Confession be made, in the name of all those that are minded to receive the holy Communion, by one of the Ministers: both he and all the people kneeling humbly upon their knees and saying,

ALMIGHTY God, Father of our Lord Jesus Christ, Maker of all things, Judge of all men: We acknowledge and bewail our manifold sins and wickedness, Which we from time to time most grievously have committed, By thought, word, and deed, Against thy Divine Majesty, Provoking most justly thy wrath and indignation against us. We do earnestly repent, And are heartily sorry for these our misdoings; The remembrance of them is grievous unto us; The burden of them is intolerable. Have mercy upon us, Have mercy upon us, most merciful Father; For thy Son our Lord Jesus Christ's sake, Forgive us all that is past; And grant that we may ever hereafter Serve and please thee In newness of life, To the honour and glory of thy Name; Through Jesus Christ our Lord. Amen.

Then shall the Priest (or the Bishop, being present,) stand up, and turning himself to the people, pronounce this Absolution

ALMIGHTY God, our heavenly Father, who of his great mercy hath promised forgiveness of sins to all them that with hearty repentance and true faith turn unto him; Have mercy upon you; pardon and deliver you from all your sins; confirm and strengthen you in all goodness; and bring you to everlasting life; through Jesus Christ our Lord. **Amen.**

Then shall the Priest say,

Hear what comfortable words our Saviour Christ saith unto all that truly turn to him.

COME unto me all that travail and are heavy laden, and I will refresh you. *S. Matth.* 11. 28.

So God loved the world, that he gave his only-begotten Son, to the end that all that believe in him should not perish, but have everlasting life. *S. John* 3. 16.

Hear also what Saint Paul saith.

This is a true saying, and worthy of all men to be received, that Christ Jesus came into the world to save sinners. *1 Tim.* 1. 15.

Hear also what Saint John saith.

If any man sin, we have an Advocate with the Father, Jesus Christ the righteous; and he is the propitiation for our sins. *1 S. John* 2. 1.

After which the Priest shall proceed, saying,

Lift up your hearts.

Answer. We lift them up unto the Lord.

Priest. Let us give thanks unto our Lord God.

Answer. It is meet and right so to do.

Then shall the Priest turn to the Lord's Table and say,

IT is very meet, right, and our bounden duty, that we should at all times, and in all places, give thanks unto thee, O Lord, *Holy Father, Almighty, Everlasting God.

*These words [**Holy Father**] must be omitted on **Trinity Sunday**.

Here shall follow the proper Preface, according to the time, if there be any specially appointed: or else immediately shall follow,

THEREFORE with Angels and Archangels, and with all the company of heaven, we laud and magnify thy glorious Name; evermore praising thee, and saying: Holy, holy, holy, Lord God of hosts, heaven and earth are full of thy glory: Glory be to thee, O Lord most High. Amen.

PROPER PREFACES

Upon **Christmas Day**, and seven days after.

BECAUSE thou didst give Jesus Christ thine only Son to be born as at this time for us; who, by the operation of the Holy Ghost, was made very man of the substance of the Virgin Mary his mother; and that without spot of sin, to make us clean from all sin. Therefore with Angels, &c.

Upon **Easter Day**, and seven days after.

BUT chiefly are we bound to praise thee for the glorious Resurrection of thy Son Jesus Christ our Lord: for he is the very Paschal Lamb, which was offered for us, and hath taken away the sin of the world; who by his death hath destroyed death, and by his rising to life again hath restored to us everlasting life. Therefore with Angels, **&c.**

Upon **Ascension Day**, and seven days after.

THROUGH thy most dearly beloved Son Jesus Christ our Lord; who after his most glorious Resurrection manifestly appeared to all his Apostles, and in their sight ascended up into heaven to prepare a place for us; that where he is, thither we might also ascend, and reign with him in glory. Therefore with Angels, **&c.**

Upon **Whitsunday**, and six days after.

THROUGH Jesus Christ our Lord; according to whose most true promise, the Holy Ghost came down as at this time from heaven with a sudden great sound, as it had been a mighty wind, in the likeness of fiery tongues, lighting upon the Apostles, to teach them, and to lead them to all truth; giving them both the gift of divers languages, and also boldness with fervent zeal constantly to preach the Gospel unto all nations; whereby we have been brought out of darkness and error into the clear light and true knowledge of thee, and of thy Son Jesus Christ. Therefore with Angels, **&c.**

Upon the Feast of **Trinity** only.

WHO art one God, one Lord; not one only Person, but three Persons in one Substance. For that which we believe of the glory of the Father, the same we believe of the Son, and of the Holy Ghost, without any difference or inequality. Therefore with Angels, **&c.**

After each of which Prefaces shall immediately be sung or said,

THEREFORE with Angels and Archangels, and with all the company of heaven, we laud and magnify thy glorious Name; evermore praising thee, and saying: Holy, holy, holy, Lord God of hosts, heaven and earth are full of thy glory: Glory be to thee, O Lord most High. Amen.

Then shall the Priest, kneeling down at the Lord's Table, say in the name of all them that shall receive the Communion this Prayer following.

WE do not presume to come to this thy Table, O merciful Lord, trusting in our own righteousness, but in thy manifold and great mercies. We are not worthy so much as to gather up the crumbs under thy Table. But thou art the same Lord, whose property is always to have mercy: Grant us therefore, gracious Lord, so to eat the flesh of thy dear Son Jesus Christ, and to drink his blood, that our sinful bodies may be made clean by his body, and our souls washed through his most precious blood, and that we may evermore dwell in him, and he in us. **Amen.**

When the Priest, standing before the Table, hath so ordered the Bread and Wine, that he may with the more readiness and decency break the Bread before the people, and take the Cup into his hands, he shall say the Prayer of Consecration, as followeth.

ALMIGHTY God, our heavenly Father, who of thy tender mercy didst give thine only Son Jesus Christ to suffer death upon the Cross for our redemption; who made there (by his one oblation of himself once offered) a full, perfect, and sufficient sacrifice, oblation, and satisfaction, for the sins of the whole world; and did institute, and in his holy Gospel command us to continue, a perpetual memory of that his precious death, until his coming again: Hear us, O merciful Father, we most humbly beseech thee; and grant that we receiving these thy creatures of bread and wine, according to thy Son our Saviour Jesus Christ's holy institution, in remembrance of his death and passion, may be partakers of his most blessed Body and Blood: who, in the same night that he was betrayed, [a]took Bread; and, when he had given thanks, [b]he brake it, and gave it to his disciples, saying, Take, eat; [c]this is my Body which is given for you: Do this in remembrance of me. Likewise after supper [d]he took the Cup; and, when he had given thanks, he gave it to them, saying,

a Here the Priest is to take the Paten into his hands:

b And here to break the Bread:

c And here to lay his hand upon all the Bread.

d Here he is to take the Cup into his hand:

Drink ye all of this; for ^ethis is my Blood of the New Testament, which is shed for you and for many for the remission of sins: Do this, as oft as ye shall drink it, in remembrance of me. **Amen.**

e And here to lay his hand upon every vessel (be it Chalice or Flagon) in which there is any Wine to be consecrated.

Then shall the Minister first receive the Communion in both kinds himself, and then proceed to deliver the same to the Bishops, Priests, and Deacons, in like manner, (if any be present,) and after that to the people also in order, into their hands, all meekly kneeling. And, when he delivereth the Bread to any one, he shall say,

THE Body of our Lord Jesus Christ, which was given for thee, preserve thy body and soul unto everlasting life: Take and eat this in remembrance that Christ died for thee, and feed on him in thy heart by faith with thanksgiving.

And the Minister that delivereth the Cup to any one shall say,

THE Blood of our Lord Jesus Christ, which was shed for thee, preserve thy body and soul unto everlasting life: Drink this in remembrance that Christ's Blood was shed for thee, and be thankful.

If the consecrated Bread or Wine be all spent before all have communicated, the Priest is to consecrate more according to the Form before prescribed: Beginning at [Our Saviour Christ in the same night, &c.] for the blessing of the Bread: and at [Likewise after Supper, &c.] for the blessing of the Cup.

When all have communicated, the Minister shall return to the Lord's Table, and reverently place upon it what remaineth of the consecrated Elements, covering the same with a fair linen cloth.

Then shall the Priest say the Lord's Prayer, the people repeating after him every petition.

OUR Father which art in heaven, Hallowed be thy Name, Thy kingdom come, Thy will be done, in earth as it is in heaven. Give us this day our daily bread; And forgive us our trespasses, As we forgive them that trespass against us; And lead us not into temptation, But deliver us from evil. For thine is the kingdom, the power, and the glory, For ever and ever. Amen.

After shall be said as followeth.

O LORD and heavenly Father, we thy humble servants entirely desire thy fatherly goodness mercifully to accept this our sacrifice of praise and thanksgiving; most humbly beseeching thee to grant, that by the merits and death of thy Son Jesus Christ, and through faith in his blood, we and all thy whole Church may obtain remission of our sins, and all other benefits of his passion. And here we offer and present unto thee, O Lord, ourselves, our souls and bodies, to be a reasonable, holy, and lively sacrifice unto thee; humbly beseeching thee, that all we, who are partakers of this holy Communion, may be fulfilled with thy grace and heavenly benediction. And although we be unworthy, through our manifold sins, to offer unto thee any sacrifice, yet we beseech thee to accept this our bounden duty and service; not weighing our merits, but pardoning our offences, through Jesus Christ our Lord; by whom, and with whom, in the unity of the Holy Ghost, all honour and glory be unto thee, O Father Almighty, world without end. **Amen.**

Or this.

ALMIGHTY and everliving God, we most heartily thank thee, for that thou dost vouchsafe to feed us, who have duly received these holy mysteries, with the spiritual food of the most precious Body and Blood of thy Son our Saviour Jesus Christ; and dost assure us thereby of thy favour and goodness towards us; and that we are very members incorporate in the mystical body of thy Son, which is the blessed company of all faithful people; and are also heirs through hope of thy everlasting kingdom, by the merits of the most precious death and passion of thy dear Son. And we most humbly beseech thee, O heavenly Father, so to assist us with thy grace, that we may continue in that holy fellowship, and do all such good works as thou hast prepared for us to walk in; through Jesus Christ our Lord, to whom, with thee and the Holy Ghost, be all honour and glory, world without end. **Amen.**

Then shall be said or sung,

GLORY be to God on high, and in earth peace, good will towards men. We praise thee, we bless thee, we worship thee, we glorify thee, we give thanks to thee for thy great glory, O Lord God, heavenly King, God the Father Almighty.

O Lord, the only-begotten Son, Jesu Christ; O Lord God, Lamb of God, Son of the Father, that takest away the sins of the world, have mercy upon us. Thou that takest away the sins of the world, have mercy upon us. Thou that takest away the sins of the world, receive our prayer. Thou that sittest at the right hand of God the Father, have mercy upon us.

For thou only art holy; thou only art the Lord; thou only, O Christ, with the Holy Ghost, art most high in the glory of God the Father. Amen.

Then the Priest (or Bishop if he be present) shall let them depart with this Blessing.

THE peace of God, which passeth all under-standing, keep your hearts and minds in the knowledge and love of God, and of his Son

Jesus Christ our Lord: And the blessing of God Almighty, the Father, the Son, and the Holy Ghost, be amongst you and remain with you always. **Amen.**

Collects to be said after the Offertory, when there is no Communion, every such day one or more; and the same may be said also, as often as occasion shall serve, after the Collects either of Morning or Evening Prayer, Communion, or Litany, by the discretion of the Minister.

ASSIST us mercifully, O Lord, in these our supplications and prayers, and dispose the way of thy servants towards the attainment of ever-lasting salvation; that, among all the changes and chances of this mortal life, they may ever be defended by thy most gracious and ready help; through Jesus Christ our Lord. **Amen.**

O ALMIGHTY Lord, and everlasting God, vouchsafe, we beseech thee, to direct, sanctify, and govern, both our hearts and bodies, in the ways of thy laws, and in the works of thy commandments; that through thy most mighty protection, both here and ever, we may be preserved in body and soul; through our Lord and Saviour Jesus Christ. **Amen.**

GRANT, we beseech thee, Almighty God, that the words, which we have heard this day with our outward ears, may through thy grace be so grafted inwardly in our hearts, that they may bring forth in us the fruit of good living, to the honour and praise of thy Name; through Jesus Christ our Lord. **Amen.**

PREVENT us, O Lord, in all our doings with thy most gracious favour, and further us with thy continual help; that in all our works, begun, continued, and ended in thee, we may glorify thy holy Name, and finally by thy mercy obtain everlasting life; through Jesus Christ our Lord. **Amen.**

ALMIGHTY God, the fountain of all wisdom, who knowest our necessities before we ask, and our ignorance in asking: We beseech thee to have compassion upon our infirmities; and those things, which for our unworthiness we dare not, and for our blindness we cannot ask, vouchsafe to give us for the worthiness of thy Son Jesus Christ our Lord. **Amen.**

ALMIGHTY God, who hast promised to hear the petitions of them that ask in thy Son's Name: We beseech thee mercifully to incline thine ears to us that have made now our prayers and supplications unto thee; and grant that those things, which we have faithfully asked according to thy will, may effectually be obtained, to the relief of our necessity, and to the setting forth of thy glory; through Jesus Christ our Lord. **Amen.**

Upon the Sundays and other Holy-days (if there be no Communion) shall be said all that is appointed at the Communion, until the end of the general Prayer [**For the whole state of Christ's Church militant here in earth**] together with one or more of these Collects last before rehearsed, concluding with the Blessing.

And there shall be no Celebration of the Lord's Supper, except there be a convenient number to communicate with the Priest, according to his discretion.

And if there be not above twenty persons in the Parish of discretion to receive the Communion: yet there shall be no Communion, except four (or three at the least) communicate with the Priest.

And in Cathedral and Collegiate Churches, and Colleges, where there are many Priests and Deacons, they shall all receive the Communion with the Priest every Sunday at the least, except they have a reasonable cause to the contrary.

And to take away all occasion of dissension, and superstition, which any person hath or might have concerning the Bread and Wine, it shall suffice that the Bread be such as is usual to be eaten; but the best and purest Wheat Bread that conveniently may be gotten.

And if any of the Bread and Wine remain unconsecrated, the Curate shall have it to his own use: but if any remain of that which was consecrated, it shall not be carried out of the Church, but the Priest, and such other of the Communicants as he shall then call unto him, shall, immediately after the Blessing, reverently eat and drink the same.

The Bread and Wine for the Communion shall be provided by the Curate and the churchwardens at the charges of the Parish.

And note, that every Parishioner shall communicate at the least three times in the year, of which Easter to be one. And yearly at Easter every Parishioner shall reckon with the Parson, Vicar, or Curate, or his or their Deputy or Deputies; and pay to them or him all Ecclesiastical Duties, accustomably due, then and at that time to be paid.

After the Divine Service ended, the money given at the Offertory shall be disposed of to such pious and charitable uses, as the Minister and churchwardens shall think fit. Wherein if they disagree, it shall be disposed of as the Ordinary shall appoint.

Whereas it is ordained in this office for the Administration of the Lord's Supper, that the Communicants should receive the same kneeling; (which order is well meant, for a signification of our humble and grateful acknowledgement of the benefits of Christ therein given to all worthy Receivers, and for the avoiding of such profanation and disorder in the holy Communion, as might otherwise ensue;) yet, lest the same kneeling should by any persons, either out of ignorance and infirmity, or out of malice and obstinacy, be misconstrued and depraved: It is here declared, that thereby no Adoration is intended, or ought to be done, either unto the Sacramental Bread or Wine there bodily received, or unto any Corporal Presence of Christ's natural Flesh and Blood. For the Sacramental Bread and Wine remain still in their very natural substances, and therefore may not be adored; (for that were Idolatry, to be abhorred of all faithful Christians;) and the natural Body and Blood of our Saviour Christ are in Heaven, and not here; it being against the truth of Christ's natural Body to be at one time in more places than one.

THE MINISTRATION OF
PUBLICK BAPTISM OF INFANTS
TO BE USED IN THE CHURCH

Due notice, normally of at least a week, shall be given before a Child is brought to the church to be baptized.

For every child to be baptized there shall be not fewer than three godparents, of whom at least two shall be of the same sex as the child and of whom at least one shall be of the opposite sex; save that, when three cannot conveniently be had, one godfather and one godmother shall suffice. Parents may be godparents for their own children provided that the child shall have at least one other godparent. The godparents shall be persons who have been baptized and confirmed and will faithfully fulfil their responsibilities both by their care for the child committed to their charge and by the example of their own godly living. Nevertheless the Minister shall have power to dispense with the requirement of confirmation in any case in which in his judgement need so requires.

The Minister shall instruct the parents or guardians of an infant to be admitted to Holy Baptism that the same responsibilities rest on them as are in the service of Holy Baptism required of the godparents.

No Minister shall refuse or, save for the purpose of preparing or instructing the parents or guardians or godparents, delay to baptize any infant within his cure that is brought to the church to be baptized, provided that due notice has been given and the provisions relating to godparents are observed. If the Minister shall refuse or unduly delay to baptize any such infant, the parents or guardians may apply to the Bishop of the diocese who shall, after consultation with the Minister, give such directions as he thinks fit.

The Minister, before proceeding to the Baptism, shall have satisfied himself that the child presented to him has not already been baptized.

At the time appointed the godfathers and godmothers and the parents or guardians with the child must be ready at the Font, and the Priest coming to the Font (which is then to be filled with pure Water,) and standing there, shall proceed as follows.

DEARLY beloved, forasmuch as all men are conceived and born in sin, and that our Saviour Christ saith, none can enter into the kingdom of God, except he be regenerate and born anew of Water and of the Holy Ghost: I beseech you to call upon God the Father, through our Lord Jesus Christ, that of his bounteous mercy he will grant to **this Child** that thing which by nature **he** cannot have; that **he** may be baptized with Water and the Holy Ghost, and received into Christ's holy Church, and be made **a lively member** of the same.

Then shall the Priest say,

Let us pray.

ALMIGHTY and everlasting God, who of thy great mercy didst save Noah and his family in the ark from perishing by water; and also didst safely lead the children of Israel thy people through the Red Sea, figuring thereby thy holy Baptism; and by the Baptism of thy well-beloved Son Jesus Christ, in the river Jordan, didst sanctify Water to the mystical washing away of sin: We beseech thee, for thine infinite mercies, that thou wilt mercifully look upon **this Child**; wash **him** and sanctify **him** with the Holy Ghost; that **he**, being delivered from thy wrath, may be received into the ark of Christ's Church; and being stedfast in faith, joyful through hope, and rooted in charity, may so pass the waves of this troublesome world, that finally **he** may come to the land of everlasting life, there to reign with thee world without end, through Jesus Christ our Lord. **Amen.**

ALMIGHTY and immortal God, the aid of all that need, the helper of all that flee to thee for succour, the life of them that believe, and the resurrection of the dead: We call upon thee for **this Infant**, that **he**, coming to thy holy Baptism, may receive remission of **his** sins by spiritual regeneration. Receive **him**, O Lord, as thou hast promised by thy well-beloved Son, saying, Ask, and ye shall have; seek, and ye shall find; knock, and it shall be opened unto you: So give now unto us that ask; let us that seek find; open the gate unto us that knock; that **this Infant** may enjoy the everlasting benediction of thy heavenly washing, and may come to the eternal kingdom which thou hast promised by Christ our Lord. **Amen.**

Then shall the people stand up, and the Priest shall say,

Hear the words of the Gospel, written by Saint Mark in the tenth chapter at the thirteenth verse.

THEY brought young children to Christ, that he should touch them; and his disciples rebuked those that brought them. But when Jesus saw it, he was much displeased, and said unto them, Suffer little children to come unto me, and forbid them not; for of such is the kingdom of God. Verily I say unto you, Whosoever shall not receive the kingdom of God as a little child, he shall not enter therein. And he took them up in his arms, put his hands upon them, and blessed them.

After the Gospel is read, the Minister shall make this brief exhortation upon the words of the Gospel.

BELOVED, ye hear in this Gospel the words of our Saviour Christ, that he commanded the children to be brought unto him; how he blamed those that would have kept them from him; how he exhorteth all men to follow their innocency. Ye perceive how by his outward gesture and deed he declared his good will toward them; for he embraced them in his arms, he laid his hands upon them, and blessed them. Doubt ye not therefore, but earnestly believe, that he will likewise favourably receive **this** present **Infant**; that he will embrace **him** with the arms of his mercy; that he will give unto **him** the blessing of eternal life, and make **him partaker** of his everlasting kingdom. Wherefore we being thus persuaded of the good will of our heavenly Father towards **this Infant**, declared by his Son Jesus Christ; and nothing doubting but that he favourably alloweth this charitable work of ours in bringing **this Infant** to his holy Baptism; let us faithfully and devoutly give thanks unto him, and say,

ALMIGHTY and everlasting God, heavenly Father, we give thee humble thanks that thou hast vouchsafed to call us to the knowledge of thy grace and faith in thee: Increase this knowledge, and confirm this faith in us evermore. Give thy Holy Spirit to **this Infant**, that **he** may be born again, and be made **an heir** of everlasting salvation, through our Lord Jesus Christ, who liveth and reigneth with thee and the Holy Spirit, now and for ever. **Amen**.

Then shall the Priest speak unto the Godfathers and Godmothers on this wise.

DEARLY beloved, ye have brought **this Child** here to be baptized; ye have prayed that our Lord Jesus Christ would vouchsafe to receive **him**, to release **him** of **his** sins, to sanctify **him** with the Holy Ghost, to give him the kingdom of heaven and everlasting life. Ye have heard also that our Lord Jesus Christ hath promised in his Gospel, to grant all these things that ye have prayed for: which promise he, for his part, will most surely keep and perform. Wherefore, after this promise made by Christ, **this Infant** must also faithfully, for **his** part, promise by you that are **his** sureties, (until **he** come of age to take it upon **himself**,) that he will renounce the devil and all his works, and constantly believe God's holy Word, and obediently keep his commandments.

I demand therefore,

DOST thou, in the name of this Child, renounce the devil and all his works, the vain pomp and glory of the world, with all covetous desires of the same, and the carnal desires of the flesh, so that thou wilt not follow nor be led by them?

Answer. I renounce them all.

Minister.

DOST thou believe in God the Father Almighty, Maker of heaven and earth?

And in Jesus Christ his only-begotten Son our Lord? And that he was conceived by the Holy Ghost, born of the Virgin Mary; that he suffered under Pontius Pilate, was crucified, dead, and buried; that he went down into hell, and also did rise again the third day; that he ascended into heaven, and sitteth at the right hand of God the Father Almighty; and from thence shall come again at the end of the world, to judge the quick and the dead?

And dost thou believe in the Holy Ghost; the holy Catholick Church; the Communion of Saints; the Remission of sins; the Resurrection of the flesh; and everlasting life after death?

Answer. All this I stedfastly believe.

Minister.

WILT thou be baptized in this faith?

Answer. That is my desire.

Minister.

WILT thou then obediently keep God's holy will and commandments, and walk in the same all the days of thy life?

Answer. I will.

Then shall the Priest say,

O MERCIFUL God, grant that the old Adam in **this Child** may be so buried, that the new man may be raised up in **him. Amen.**

Grant that all carnal affections may die in **him**, and that all things belonging to the Spirit may live and grow in **him. Amen.**

Grant that **he** may have power and strength, to have victory, and to triumph against the devil, the world, and the flesh. **Amen.**

Grant that whosoever is here dedicated to thee by our office and ministry may also be endued with heavenly virtues, and everlastingly rewarded, through thy mercy, O blessed

Lord God, who dost live, and govern all things, world without end. **Amen.**

ALMIGHTY everliving God, whose most dearly beloved Son Jesus Christ, for the forgiveness of our sins, did shed out of his most precious side both water and blood; and gave commandment to his disciples, that they should go teach all nations, and baptize them in the Name of the Father, and of the Son, and of the Holy Ghost: Regard, we beseech thee, the supplications of thy Congregation; sanctify this Water to the mystical washing away of sin; and grant that **this Child**, now to be baptized therein, may receive the fulness of thy grace, and ever remain in the number of thy faithful and elect children; through Jesus Christ our Lord. **Amen.**

Then the Priest shall take the Child into his hands, and shall say to the Godfathers and Godmothers, Name this Child. And then naming it after them (if they shall certify him that the Child may well endure it) he shall dip it in the Water discreetly and warily, saying,

N. I baptize thee in the Name of the Father, and of the Son, and of the Holy Ghost. Amen.

But if they certify that the Child is weak, it shall suffice to pour Water upon it, saying the foresaid words,

N. I baptize thee in the Name of the Father, and of the Son, and of the Holy Ghost. Amen.

Then the Priest shall say,

WE receive this Child into the Congregation of Christ's flock, *and do sign **him** with the sign of the Cross, in token that hereafter **he** shall not be ashamed to confess the faith of Christ crucified, and manfully to fight under his banner against sin, the world, and the devil, and to continue Christ's faithful soldier and servant unto **his** life's end. Amen.

Then shall the Priest say,

SEEING now, dearly beloved brethren, that **this Child** is regenerate and grafted into the body of Christ's Church, let us give thanks unto Almighty God for these benefits, and with one accord make our prayers unto him, that **this**

[*Here the Priest shall make a Cross upon the Child's forehead.]

Child may lead the rest of **his** life according to this beginning.

Then shall be said, all kneeling,

OUR Father which art in heaven, Hallowed be thy Name, Thy kingdom come, Thy will be done, in earth as it is in heaven. Give us this day our daily bread; And forgive us our trespasses, As we forgive them that trespass against us; And lead us not into temptation, But deliver us from evil. Amen.

Then shall the Priest say,

WE yield thee hearty thanks, most merciful Father, that it hath pleased thee to regenerate **this Infant** with thy Holy Spirit, to receive **him** for thine own **Child** by adoption, and to incorporate **him** into thy holy Church. And humbly we beseech thee to grant that **he** being dead unto sin, and living unto righteousness, and being buried with Christ in his death, may crucify the old man, and utterly abolish the whole body of sin; and that, as **he is** made **partaker** of the death of thy Son, **he** may also be **partaker** of his resurrection; so that finally, with the residue of thy holy Church, **he** may be **an inheritor** of thine everlasting kingdom; through Christ our Lord. **Amen.**

Then, all standing up, the Priest shall say to the Godfathers and Godmothers this exhortation following.

FORASMUCH as **this Child hath** promised by you **his** sureties to renounce the devil and all his works, to believe in God, and to serve him: Ye must remember that it is your parts and duties to see that **this Infant** be taught, so soon as **he** shall be able to learn, what a solemn vow, promise and profession **he hath** here made by you. And that **he** may know these things the better, ye shall call upon him to hear sermons; and chiefly ye shall provide that he may learn the Creed, the Lord's Prayer and the Ten Commandments in the vulgar tongue, and all other things which a Christian ought to know and believe to his soul's health; and that **this Child** may be virtuously brought up to lead a godly and a Christian life; remembering always, that Baptism doth represent unto us our profession; which is, to follow the example of our Saviour Christ, and to be made like unto him; that as he died and rose again for us, so should we, who are baptized, die from sin and rise again unto righteousness, continually mortifying all our evil and corrupt affections, and daily proceeding in all virtue and godliness of living.

Then shall he add and say,

YE are to take care that **this Child** be brought to the Bishop to be confirmed by him, so soon as **he** can say the Creed, the Lord's Prayer and the Ten Commandments in the vulgar tongue, and be further instructed in the Church Catechism set forth for that purpose.

It is certain by God's Word, that children which are baptized, dying before they commit actual sin, are undoubtedly saved.

To take away all scruple concerning the use of the sign of the Cross in Baptism; the true explication thereof, and the just reasons for the retaining of it, may be seen in the xxxth Canon, first published in the year MDCIV.

THE MINISTRATION OF
PRIVATE BAPTISM
OF CHILDREN
IN HOUSES

The Minister of every parish shall warn the people that without great cause and necessity they procure not their children to be baptized at home in their houses. But when need shall compel them so to do, then Baptism shall be administered on this fashion.

First let the Minister of the Parish (or, in his absence, any other lawful Minister that can be procured) with them that are present call upon God, and say the Lord's Prayer, and so many of the Collects appointed to be said before in the form of Publick Baptism, as the time and present exigence will suffer. And then, the child being named by some one that is present, the Minister shall pour Water upon it, saying these words;

N. I baptize thee in the Name of the Father, and of the Son, and of the Holy Ghost. Amen.

Then, all kneeling down, the Minister shall give thanks unto God, and say,

WE yield thee hearty thanks, most merciful Father, that it hath pleased thee to regenerate this Infant with thy Holy Spirit, to receive **him** for thine own Child by adoption, and to incorporate **him** into thy holy Church. And we humbly beseech thee to grant, that as **he** is now made partaker of the death of thy Son, so **he** may be also of his resurrection; and that finally, with the residue of thy Saints, **he** may inherit thine everlasting kingdom; through the same thy Son Jesus Christ our Lord. **Amen.**

And let them not doubt, but that the Child so baptized is lawfully and sufficiently baptized, and ought not to be baptized again. Yet nevertheless, if the Child which is after this sort baptized do afterward live, it is expedient that it be brought into the Church, to the intent that, if the Minister of the same Parish did himself baptize that Child, the Congregation may be certified of the true form of Baptism, by him privately before used. In which case he shall say thus,

I CERTIFY you, that according to the due and prescribed Order of the Church, **at such a time, and at such a place**, before divers witnesses, I baptized this Child.

But if the Child were baptized by any other lawful Minister, then the Minister of the Parish, where the Child

was born or christened, shall examine and try whether the Child be lawfully baptized, or no. In which case, if those that bring any Child to the Church do answer that the same Child is already baptized, then shall the Minister examine them further, saying,

BY whom was this Child baptized?

Who was present when this Child was baptized?

Because some things essential to this Sacrament may happen to be omitted through fear or haste, in such times of extremity; therefore I demand further of you,

With what matter was this Child baptized?

With what words was this Child baptized?

And if the Minister shall find by the answers of such as bring the Child, that all things were done as they ought to be; then shall not he christen the Child again, but shall receive him as one of the flock of true Christian people, saying thus,

I CERTIFY you, that in this case all is well done, and according unto due order, concerning the baptizing of this Child; who being born in original sin, and in the wrath of God, is now, by the laver of Regeneration in Baptism, received into the number of the children of God and heirs of everlasting life: for our Lord Jesus Christ doth not deny his grace and mercy unto such infants, but most lovingly doth call them unto him, as the holy Gospel doth witness to our comfort on this wise.

S. MARK 10. 13

THEY brought young children to Christ, that he should touch them; and his disciples rebuked those that brought them. But when Jesus saw it, he was much displeased, and said unto them, Suffer the little children to come unto me, and forbid them not; for of such is the kingdom of God. Verily I say unto you, Whosoever shall not receive the kingdom of God as a little child, he shall not enter therein. And he took them up in his arms, put his hands upon them, and blessed them.

After the Gospel is read, the Minister shall make this brief exhortation upon the words of the Gospel.

BELOVED, ye hear in this Gospel the words of our Saviour Christ, that he commanded the children to be brought unto him; how he blamed those that would have kept them from him; how he exhorted all men to follow their innocency. Ye perceive how by his outward gesture and deed he declared his good will toward them; for he embraced them in his arms, he laid his hands upon them, and blessed them. Doubt ye not therefore, but earnestly believe, that he hath likewise favourably received this present Infant; that he hath embraced **him** with the arms of his mercy; and (as he hath promised in his holy Word) will give unto **him** the blessing of eternal life, and make **him** partaker of his everlasting kingdom. Wherefore, we being thus persuaded of the good will of our heavenly Father, declared by his Son Jesus Christ, towards this Infant, let us faithfully and devoutly give thanks unto him, and say the Prayer which the Lord himself taught us:

OUR Father which art in heaven, Hallowed be thy Name, Thy kingdom come, Thy will be done, in earth as it is in heaven. Give us this day our daily bread; And forgive us our trespasses, As we forgive them that trespass against us; And lead us not into temptation, But deliver us from evil. Amen.

ALMIGHTY and everlasting God, heavenly Father, we give thee humble thanks that thou hast vouchsafed to call us to the knowledge of thy grace and faith in thee: Increase this knowledge, and confirm this faith in us evermore. Give thy Holy Spirit to this Infant, that **he**, being born again, and being made an heir of everlasting salvation, through our Lord Jesus Christ, may continue thy servant, and attain thy promise; through the same our Lord Jesus Christ thy Son, who liveth and reigneth with thee and the Holy Spirit, now and for ever. **Amen.**

Then shall the Priest demand the Name of the Child; which being by the Godfathers and Godmothers pronounced, the Minister shall say,

DOST thou, in the name of this Child, renounce the devil and all his works, the vain pomp and glory of this world, with all covetous desires of the same, and the carnal desires of the flesh, so that thou wilt not follow nor be led by them?

Answer. I renounce them all.

Minister.

DOST thou believe in God the Father Almighty, Maker of heaven and earth?

And in Jesus Christ his only-begotten Son our Lord? And that he was conceived by the Holy Ghost, born of the Virgin Mary; that he suffered under Pontius Pilate, was crucified, dead, and buried; that he went down into hell, and also did rise again the third day; that he ascended into heaven, and sitteth at the right hand of God the Father Almighty; and from thence shall come again at the end of the world, to judge the quick and the dead?

And dost thou believe in the Holy Ghost; the holy Catholick Church; the Communion of Saints; the Remission of sins; the Resurrection of the flesh; and everlasting life after death?

Answer. All this I stedfastly believe.

Minister.

WILT thou then obediently keep God's holy will and commandments, and walk in the same all the days of thy life?

Answer. I will.

Then the Priest shall say,

WE receive this Child into the Congregation of Christ's flock, and do *sign **him** with the sign of the Cross, in token that hereafter **he** shall not be ashamed to confess the faith of Christ crucified, and manfully to fight under his banner against sin, the world, and the devil, and to continue Christ's faithful soldier and servant unto **his** life's end. Amen.

Then shall the Priest say,

SEEING now, dearly beloved brethren, that this Child is by Baptism regenerate and grafted into the body of Christ's Church, let us give thanks unto Almighty God for these benefits,

[*The Priest shall make a Cross upon the Child's forehead.]

and with one accord make our prayers unto him, that **he** may lead the rest of **his** life according to this beginning.

Then shall the Priest say,

WE yield thee most hearty thanks, most merciful Father, that it hath pleased thee to regenerate this Infant with thy Holy Spirit, to receive **him** for thine own Child by adoption, and to incorporate **him** into thy holy Church. And humbly we beseech thee to grant that **he** being dead unto sin, and living unto righteousness, and being buried with Christ in his death, may crucify the old man, and utterly abolish the whole body of sin; and that, as **he** is made partaker of the death of thy Son, **he** may also be partaker of his resurrection; so that finally, with the residue of thy holy Church, **he** may be an inheritor of thine everlasting kingdom; through Jesus Christ our Lord. **Amen.**

Then, all standing up, the Minister shall make this exhortation to the Godfathers and Godmothers.

FORASMUCH as this Child hath promised by

you **his** sureties to renounce the devil and all his works, to believe in God, and to serve him: Ye must remember, that it is your parts and duties to see that this Infant be taught, so soon as **he** shall be able to learn, what a solemn vow, promise and profession **he** hath made by you. And that **he** may know these things the better, ye shall call upon **him** to hear sermons; and chiefly ye shall provide that **he** may learn the Creed, the Lord's Prayer and the Ten Commandments in the vulgar tongue, and all other things which a Christian ought to know and believe to his soul's health; and that this Child may be virtuously brought up to lead a godly and a Christian life; remembering alway, that Baptism doth represent unto us our profession; which is, to follow the example of our Saviour Christ, and be made like unto him; that as he died and rose again for us, so should we, who are baptized, die from sin and rise again unto righteousness, continually mortifying all our evil and corrupt affections, and daily proceeding in all virtue and godliness of living.

But if they which bring the Infant to the Church do make such uncertain answers to the Priest's questions, as that it cannot appear that the Child was baptized with Water, In the Name of the Father, and of the Son, and of the Holy Ghost, (which are essential parts of Baptism,) then let the Priest baptize it in the form before appointed for Publick Baptism of Infants: Saving that at the dipping of the Child in the Font, he shall use this form of words.

IF thou art not already baptized, **N.** I baptize thee in the Name of the Father, and of the Son, and of the Holy Ghost. Amen.

THE MINISTRATION OF
BAPTISM
TO SUCH AS ARE OF RIPER YEARS AND ABLE TO ANSWER FOR THEMSELVES

When any such person as is of riper years and able to answer for himself is to be baptized, the Minister shall instruct such person, or cause him to be instructed, in the principles of the Christian religion, and exhort him so to prepare himself with prayers and fasting that he may receive this Holy Sacrament with repentance and faith.

At least a week before any such baptism is to take place, the Minister shall give notice thereof to the Bishop of the Diocese or whomsoever he shall appoint for the purpose.

The person to be baptized shall choose three, or at least two, to be his sponsors, who shall be ready to present him at the Font and afterwards put him in mind of his Christian profession and duties. No person shall be admitted to be a sponsor who has not been baptized and confirmed. Nevertheless the Minister shall have power to dispense with the requirement of confirmation in any case in which in his judgement need so requires.

At the time appointed, the sponsors shall be ready to present the person to be baptized at the Font, and standing there the Priest shall ask whether the person

presented be baptized or no, and if he shall answer, No, then shall the Priest say thus.

DEARLY beloved, forasmuch as all men are conceived and born in sin, (and that which is born of the flesh is flesh,) and they that are in the flesh cannot please God, but live in sin, committing many actual transgressions; and that our Saviour Christ saith, none can enter into the kingdom of God, except he be regenerate and born anew of Water and of the Holy Ghost; I beseech you to call upon God the Father, through our Lord Jesus Christ, that of his bounteous goodness he will grant to **these persons** that which by nature **they** cannot have; that they may be baptized with Water and the Holy Ghost, and received into Christ's holy Church, and be made lively **members** of the same.

Then shall the Priest say,

Let us pray.

(And here all the Congregation shall kneel.)

ALMIGHTY and everlasting God, who of thy great mercy didst save Noah and his family in the ark from perishing by water; and also didst safely lead the children of Israel thy people through the Red Sea, figuring thereby thy holy Baptism; and by the Baptism of thy well-beloved Son Jesus Christ, in the river Jordan, didst sanctify the element of water to the mystical washing away of sin: We beseech thee, for thine infinite mercies, that thou wilt mercifully look upon **these** thy **servants**; wash **them** and sanctify **them** with the Holy Ghost; that **they**, being delivered from thy wrath, may be received into the ark of Christ's Church; and being stedfast in faith, joyful through hope, and rooted in charity, may so pass the waves of this troublesome world, that finally **they** may come to the land of everlasting life, there to reign with thee world without end, through Jesus Christ our Lord. **Amen.**

ALMIGHTY and immortal God, the aid of all that need, the helper of all that flee to thee for succour, the life of them that believe, and the resurrection of the dead: We call upon thee for **these persons**, that **they**, coming to thy holy Baptism, may receive remission of **their** sins by spiritual regeneration. Receive **them**, O Lord: and as thou hast promised by thy well-beloved Son, saying, Ask, and ye shall receive; seek, and ye shall find; knock, and it shall be opened unto you: So give now unto us that ask; let us that seek find; open the gate unto us that knock; that **these persons** may enjoy the everlasting benediction of thy heavenly washing, and may come to the eternal kingdom which thou hast promised by Christ our Lord. **Amen.**

Then shall the people stand up, and the Priest shall say,

Hear the words of the Gospel, written by Saint John in the third chapter, beginning at the first verse.

THERE was a man of the Pharisees, named Nicodemus, a ruler of the Jews. The same came to Jesus by night, and said unto him, Rabbi, we know that thou art a teacher come from God;

for no man can do these miracles that thou doest, except God be with him. Jesus answered and said unto him, Verily, verily I say unto thee, Except a man be born again, he cannot see the kingdom of God. Nicodemus saith unto him, How can a man be born when he is old? Can he enter the second time into his mother's womb, and be born? Jesus answered, Verily, verily I say unto thee, Except a man be born of water and of the Spirit, he cannot enter into the kingdom of God. That which is born of the flesh is flesh; and that which is born of the Spirit is spirit. Marvel not that I said unto thee, Ye must be born again. The wind bloweth where it listeth, and thou hearest the sound thereof; but canst not tell whence it cometh, and whither it goeth: so is every one that is born of the Spirit.

After which he shall say this exhortation following.

BELOVED, ye hear in this Gospel the express words of our Saviour Christ, that except a man be born of water and of the Spirit, he cannot enter into the kingdom of God. Whereby ye may perceive the great necessity of this Sacrament, where it may be had. Likewise, immediately before his ascension into heaven, (as we read in the last chapter of Saint Mark's Gospel,) he gave command to his disciples, saying, Go ye into all the world, and preach the Gospel to every creature. He that believeth and is baptized shall be saved; but he that believeth not shall be damned. Which also sheweth unto us the great benefit we reap thereby. For which cause Saint Peter the Apostle, when upon his first preaching of the Gospel many were pricked at the heart, and said to him and the rest of the Apostles, Men and brethren, what shall we do? replied and said unto them, Repent, and be baptized every one of you for the remission of sins, and ye shall receive the gift of the Holy Ghost. For the promise is to you and your children, and to all that are afar off, even as many as the Lord our God shall call. And with many other words exhorted he them, saying, Save yourselves from this untoward generation. For (as the same Apostle testifieth in another place) even Baptism doth also now save us, (not the putting away of the filth of the flesh, but the answer of a good conscience towards God,) by the resurrection of Jesus Christ. Doubt ye not therefore, but earnestly believe, that he will favourably receive **these** present **persons**, truly repenting, and coming unto him by faith; that he will grant **them** remission of their sins, and bestow upon **them** the Holy Ghost; that he will give **them** the blessing of eternal life, and make **them partakers** of his everlasting kingdom. Wherefore we being thus persuaded of the good will of our heavenly Father towards **these persons**, declared by his Son Jesus Christ; let us faithfully and devoutly give thanks to him, and say,

ALMIGHTY and everlasting God, heavenly Father, we give thee humble thanks, for that thou hast vouchsafed to call us to the knowledge of thy grace and faith in thee: Increase this knowledge, and confirm this faith in us evermore. Give thy Holy Spirit to **these persons**, that **they** may be born again, and be made **heirs** of everlasting salvation, through our Lord Jesus Christ, who liveth and reigneth with thee and the Holy Spirit, now and for ever. **Amen.**

Then the Priest shall speak to the persons to be baptized on this wise.

WELL-BELOVED, who are come hither desiring to receive holy Baptism, ye have heard how the Congregation hath prayed that our Lord Jesus Christ would vouchsafe to receive you and bless you, to release you of yoursins, to give you the kingdom of heaven and everlasting life. **Ye** have heard also that our Lord Jesus Christ hath promised in his holy Word, to grant all those things that we have prayed for; which promise he, for his part, will most surely keep and perform. Wherefore, after this promise made by Christ, **ye** must also faithfully, for your part, promise in the presence of these your witnesses, and this whole Congregation, that **ye** will renounce the devil and all his works, and constantly believe God's holy Word, and obediently keep his commandments.

Then shall the Priest demand of each of the persons to be baptized, severally, these Questions following.

Question.

DOST thou renounce the devil and all his works, the vain pomp and glory of the world, with all covetous desires of the same, and the carnal desires of the flesh, so that thou wilt not follow nor be led by them?

Answer. I renounce them all.

Question.

DOST thou believe in God the Father Almighty, Maker of heaven and earth?

And in Jesus Christ his only-begotten Son our Lord? And that he was conceived by the Holy Ghost, born of the Virgin Mary; that he suffered under Pontius Pilate, was crucified, dead, and buried; that he went down into hell, and also did rise again the third day; that he ascended into heaven, and sitteth at the right hand of God the Father Almighty; and from thence shall come again at the end of the world, to judge the quick and the dead?

And dost thou believe in the Holy Ghost; the holy Catholick Church; the Communion of Saints; the Remission of sins; the Resurrection of the flesh; and everlasting life after death?

Answer. All this I stedfastly believe.

Question.

WILT thou be baptized in this faith?
Answer. That is my desire.

Question.

WILT thou then obediently keep God's holy will and commandments, and walk in the same all the days of thy life?

Answer. I will endeavour so to do, God being my helper.

Then shall the Priest say,

O MERCIFUL God, grant that the old Adam **in**

these persons may be so buried, that the new man may be raised up in them. **Amen.**

Grant that all carnal affections may die in **them**, and that all things belonging to the Spirit may live and grow in **them. Amen.**

Grant that **they** may have power and strength, to have victory, and to triumph against the devil, the world, and the flesh. **Amen.**

Grant that **they**, being here dedicated to thee by our office and ministry, may also be endued with heavenly virtues, and everlastingly rewarded, through thy mercy, O blessed Lord God, who dost live, and govern all things, world without end. **Amen.**

ALMIGHTY everliving God, whose most dearly beloved Son Jesus Christ, for the forgiveness of our sins, did shed out of his most precious side both water and blood; and gave commandment to his disciples, that they should go teach all nations, and baptize them in the Name of the Father, the Son, and the Holy Ghost:

Regard, we beseech thee, the supplications of this Congregation; sanctify this Water to the mystical washing away of sin; and grant that the **persons** now to be baptized therein may receive the fulness of thy grace, and ever remain in the number of thy faithful and elect children; through Jesus Christ our Lord. **Amen**.

Then shall the Priest take each person to be baptized by the right hand, and placing him conveniently by the Font, according to his discretion, shall ask the Godfathers and Godmothers the Name; and then shall dip him in the water, or pour water upon him, saying,

N. I baptize thee, In the Name of the Father, and of the Son, and of the Holy Ghost. Amen.

Then shall the Priest say,

WE receive this person into the Congregation of Christ's flock; and *do sign **him** with the sign of the Cross, in token that hereafter he shall not be ashamed to confess the faith of Christ crucified, and manfully to fight under his

[*Here the Priest shall make a Cross upon the person's forehead.]

banner against sin, the world, and the devil, and to continue Christ's faithful soldier and servant unto **his** life's end. Amen.

Then shall the Priest say,

SEEING now, dearly beloved brethren, that **these persons are** regenerate and grafted into the body of Christ's Church, let us give thanks unto Almighty God for these benefits, and with one accord make our prayers unto him, that they may lead the rest of **their** life according to this beginning.

Then shall be said the Lord's Prayer, all kneeling.

OUR Father which art in heaven, Hallowed be thy Name, Thy kingdom come, Thy will be done, in earth as it is in heaven. Give us this day our daily bread; And forgive us our trespasses, As we forgive them that trespass against us; And lead us not into temptation, But deliver us from evil. Amen.

WE yield thee humble thanks, O heavenly Father, that thou hast vouchsafed to call us to the knowledge of thy grace and faith in thee; Increase this knowledge, and confirm this faith in us evermore. Give thy Holy Spirit to **these persons**; that, being now born again, and made **heirs** of everlasting salvation, through our Lord Jesus Christ, **they** may continue thy **servants**, and attain thy promises; through the same Lord Jesus Christ thy Son, who liveth and reigneth with thee, in the unity of the same Holy Spirit, everlastingly. **Amen.**

Then, all standing up, the Priest shall use this exhortation following; speaking to the Godfathers and Godmothers first.

FORASMUCH as **these persons have** promised in your presence to renounce the devil and all his works, to believe in God, and to serve him: Ye must remember that it is your part and duty to put **them** in mind, what a solemn vow, promise, and profession **they** have now made before this Congregation, and especially before you **their** chosen witnesses. And ye are also to call upon **them** to use all diligence to be rightly instructed in God's holy Word; that so

they may grow in grace, and in the knowledge of our Lord Jesus Christ, and live godly, righteously, and soberly in this present world.

(And then, speaking to the new baptized **persons**, he shall proceed, and say,)

AND as for you, who have now by Baptism put on Christ, it is your part and duty also, being made the **children** of God and of the light by faith in Jesus Christ, to walk answerably to your Christian calling, and as becometh the children of light; remembering always, that Baptism representeth unto us our profession; which is, to follow the example of our Saviour Christ, and to be made like unto him; that as he died and rose again for us, so should we, who are baptized, die from sin and rise again unto righteousness, continually mortifying all our evil and corrupt affections, and daily proceeding in all virtue and godliness of living.

It is expedient that every person, thus baptized, should be confirmed by the Bishop so soon after his Baptism as conveniently may be; that so he may be admitted to the holy Communion.

If any persons not baptized in their infancy shall be brought to be baptized before they come to years of discretion to answer for themselves; it may suffice to use the Office for Publick Baptism of Infants, or (in case of extreme danger) the Office for Private Baptism; only changing the word [**Infant**] for [**Child** or **Person**] as occasion requireth.

A CATECHISM

THAT IS TO SAY

AN INSTRUCTION TO BE LEARNED OF EVERY PERSON BEFORE HE BE BROUGHT TO BE CONFIRMED BY THE BISHOP

QUESTION. What is your Name?

Answer. N. or M.

Question. Who gave you this Name?

Answer. My Godfathers and Godmothers in my Baptism; wherein I was made a member of Christ, the child of God, and an inheritor of the kingdom of heaven.

Question. What did your Godfathers and Godmothers then for you?

Answer. They did promise and vow three things in my name. First, that I should renounce the devil and all his works, the pomps and vanity of this wicked world, and all the sinful lusts of the flesh. Secondly, that I should believe all the articles of the Christian faith. And thirdly, that I should keep God's holy will and commandments, and walk in the same all the days of my life.

Question. Dost thou not think that thou art bound to believe, and to do, as they have promised for thee?

Answer. Yes verily: and by God's help so I will. And I heartily thank our heavenly Father, that he hath called me to this state of salvation, through Jesus Christ our Saviour. And I pray unto God to give me his grace, that I may continue in the same unto my life's end.

Catechist.

Rehearse the Articles of thy Belief.

Answer.

I BELIEVE in God the Father Almighty, Maker of heaven and earth:

And in Jesus Christ his only Son our Lord, Who was conceived by the Holy Ghost, Born of the Virgin Mary, Suffered under Pontius Pilate, Was crucified, dead, and buried: He descended into hell; The third day he rose again from the dead; He ascended into heaven, And sitteth at the right hand of God the Father Almighty;

From thence he shall come to judge the quick and the dead.

I believe in the Holy Ghost; The holy Catholick Church; The Communion of Saints; The Forgiveness of sins; The Resurrection of the body, And the life everlasting. Amen.

Question. What dost thou chiefly learn in these Articles of thy Belief?

Answer. First, I learn to believe in God the Father, who hath made me, and all the world.

Secondly, in God the Son, who hath redeemed me, and all mankind.

Thirdly, in God the Holy Ghost, who sanctifieth me, and all the elect people of God.

Question.

You said that your Godfathers and Godmothers did promise for you, that you should keep God's Commandments. Tell me how many there be?

Answer. Ten.

Question. Which be they?

Answer.

THE same which God spake in the twentieth chapter of Exodus, saying, I am the Lord thy God, who brought thee out of the land of Egypt, out of the house of bondage.

I. Thou shalt have none other gods but me.

II. Thou shalt not make to thyself any graven image, nor the likeness of any thing that is in heaven above, or in the earth beneath, or in the water under the earth. Thou shalt not bow down to them, nor worship them. For I the Lord thy God am a jealous God, and visit the sins of the fathers upon the children unto the third and fourth generation of them that hate me, and shew mercy unto thousands in them that love me and keep my commandments.

III. Thou shalt not take the Name of the Lord thy God in vain: for the Lord will not hold him guiltless, that taketh his Name in vain.

IV. Remember that thou keep holy the Sabbath day. Six days shalt thou labour, and do all that thou hast to do; but the seventh day is the Sabbath of the Lord thy God. In it thou shalt do no manner of work, thou, and thy son, and thy daughter, thy man-servant, and thy maid-servant, thy cattle, and the stranger that is within thy gates. For in six days the Lord made heaven and earth, the sea, and all that in them is, and rested the seventh day: wherefore the Lord blessed the seventh day, and hallowed it.

V. Honour thy father and thy mother; that thy days may be long in the land which the Lord thy God giveth thee.

VI. Thou shalt do no murder.

VII. Thou shalt not commit adultery.

VIII. Thou shalt not steal.

IX. Thou shalt not bear false witness against thy neighbour.

X. Thou shalt not covet thy neighbour's house, thou shalt not covet thy neighbour's wife, nor his servant, nor his maid, nor his ox, nor his ass, nor any thing that is his.

Question.

What dost thou chiefly learn by these Commandments?

Answer. I learn two things: my duty towards God, and my duty towards my Neighbour.

Question. What is thy duty towards God?

Answer. My duty towards God is to believe in him, to fear him, and to love him, with all my heart, with all my mind, with all my soul, and with all my strength; to worship him, to give him thanks, to put my whole trust in him, to call upon him, to honour his holy Name and his Word, and to serve him truly all the days of my life.

Question. What is thy duty towards thy Neighbour?

Answer. My duty towards my Neighbour is to love him as myself, and to do to all men as I would they should do unto me: To love, honour, and succour my father and mother: To honour and obey the Queen, and all that are put in authority under her: To submit myself to all my governors, teachers, spiritual pastors and masters: To order myself lowly and reverently to all my betters: To hurt nobody by word nor deed: To be true and just in all my dealing: To bear no malice nor hatred in my heart: To keep my hands from picking and stealing, and my tongue from evil-speaking, lying, and slandering: To keep my body in temperance, soberness, and chastity: Not to covet nor desire other men's goods; but to learn and labour truly to get mine own living, and to do my duty in that state of life, unto which it shall please God to call me.

Catechist.

My good child, know this, that thou art not able to do these things of thyself, nor to walk in the commandments of God, and to serve him, without his special grace; which thou must learn at all times to call for by diligent prayer. Let me hear therefore if thou canst say the Lord's Prayer.

Answer.

OUR Father which art in heaven, Hallowed be thy Name, Thy kingdom come, Thy will be done, in earth as it is in heaven. Give us this day our daily bread; And forgive us our trespasses, As we forgive them that trespass against us; And lead us not into temptation, But deliver us from evil. Amen.

Question. What desirest thou of God in this Prayer?

Answer. I desire my Lord God our heavenly Father, who is the giver of all goodness, to send his grace unto me, and to all people, that we may worship him, serve him, and obey him, as we ought to do. And I pray unto God, that he will send us all things that be needful both for our souls and bodies; and that he will be merciful unto us, and forgive us our sins; and that it will please him to save and defend us in all dangers ghostly and bodily; and that he will keep us from all sin and wickedness, and from our ghostly enemy, and from everlasting death. And this I trust he will do of his mercy and goodness, through our Lord Jesus Christ. And therefore I say, Amen, So be it.

Question.

HOW many Sacraments hath Christ ordained in his Church?

Answer. Two only, as generally necessary to salvation; that is to say, Baptism, and the Supper of the Lord.

Question. What meanest thou by this word **Sacrament?**

Answer. I mean an outward and visible sign of an inward and spiritual grace given unto us, ordained by Christ himself, as a means whereby we receive the same, and a pledge to assure us thereof.

Question. How many parts are there in a Sacrament?

Answer. Two: the outward visible sign, and the inward spiritual grace.

Question. What is the outward visible sign or form in Baptism?

Answer. Water: wherein the person is baptized, **In the Name of the Father, and of the Son, and of the Holy Ghost.**

Question. What is the inward and spiritual grace?

Answer. A death unto sin, and a new birth unto righteousness: for being by nature born in sin, and the children of wrath, we are hereby made the children of grace.

Question. What is required of persons to be baptized?

Answer. Repentance, whereby they forsake sin: and faith, whereby they stedfastly believe the promises of God, made to them in that Sacrament.

Question. Why then are infants baptized, when by reason of their tender age they cannot perform them?

Answer. Because they promise them both by their sureties: which promise, when they come to age, themselves are bound to perform.

Question. Why was the Sacrament of the Lord's Supper ordained?

Answer. For the continual remembrance of

the sacrifice of the death of Christ, and of the benefits which we receive thereby.

Question. What is the outward part or sign of the Lord's Supper?

Answer. Bread and Wine, which the Lord hath commanded to be received.

Question. What is the inward part, or thing signified?

Answer. The Body and Blood of Christ, which are verily and indeed taken and received by the faithful in the Lord's Supper.

Question. What are the benefits whereof we are partakers thereby?

Answer. The strengthening and refreshing of our souls by the Body and Blood of Christ, as our bodies are by the Bread and Wine.

Question. What is required of them who come to the Lord's Supper?

Answer. To examine themselves, whether they repent them truly of their former sins, stedfastly purposing to lead a new life; have a lively faith in God's mercy through Christ, with a thankful remembrance of his death; and be in charity with all men.

The Curate of every Parish shall diligently upon Sundays and Holy-days, after the second Lesson at Evening Prayer, openly in the Church instruct and examine so many Children of his Parish sent unto him, as he shall think convenient, in some part of this Catechism.

And all Fathers, Mothers, Masters, and Dames, shall cause their Children, Servants, and Prentices, (which have not learned their Catechism,) to come to the Church at the time appointed, and obediently to hear and be ordered by the Curate, until such time as they have learned all that is here appointed for them to learn.

So soon as Children are come to a competent age, and can say, in their mother tongue, the Creed, the Lord's Prayer, and the Ten Commandments; and also can answer to the other questions of this short Catechism; they shall be brought to the Bishop: And every one shall have a Godfather, or a Godmother, as a witness of their Confirmation.

And whensoever the Bishop shall give knowledge for Children to be brought unto him for their Confirmation, the Curate of every Parish shall either bring or send in writing, with his hand subscribed thereunto, the names of all such persons within his Parish, as he shall think fit to be presented to the Bishop to be confirmed. And, if the Bishop approve of them, he shall confirm them in manner following.

THE ORDER OF
CONFIRMATION
OR LAYING ON OF HANDS UPON THOSE THAT ARE BAPTIZED AND COME TO YEARS OF DISCRETION

Upon the day appointed, all that are to be then confirmed, being placed, and standing in order before the Bishop; he (or some other Minister appointed by him) shall read this Preface following.

TO the end that Confirmation may be ministered to the more edifying of such as shall receive it, the Church hath thought good to order, That none hereafter shall be confirmed, but such as can say the Creed, the Lord's Prayer, and the Ten Commandments; and can also answer to such other Questions, as in the short Catechism are contained: which order is very convenient to be observed; to the end that children being now come to the years of discretion, and having learned what their Godfathers and Godmothers promised for them in Baptism, they may themselves, with their own mouth and consent, openly before the Church, ratify and confirm the same; and also promise, that by the grace of God they will evermore endeavour themselves faithfully to observe such things, as they by their own confession have assented unto.

Then shall the Bishop say,

DO ye here, in the presence of God, and of this Congregation, renew the solemn promise and vow that was made in your name at your Baptism; ratifying and confirming the same in your own persons, and acknowledging yourselves bound to believe and to do all those things, which your Godfathers and Godmothers then undertook for you?

And every one shall audibly answer,
I do.

The Bishop.

OUR help is in the Name of the Lord;
    Answer. Who hath made heaven and earth.
    Bishop. Blessed be the Name of the Lord;

Answer. Henceforth world without end.
Bishop. Lord, hear our prayers.
Answer. And let our cry come unto thee.

Bishop.
Let us pray.

ALMIGHTY and everliving God, who hast vouchsafed to regenerate these thy servants by Water and the Holy Ghost, and hast given unto them forgiveness of all their sins: Strengthen them, we beseech thee, O Lord, with the Holy Ghost the Comforter, and daily increase in them thy manifold gifts of grace; the spirit of wisdom and understanding; the spirit of counsel and ghostly strength; the spirit of knowledge and true godliness; and fill them, O Lord, with the spirit of thy holy fear, now and for ever. **Amen.**

Then all of them in order kneeling before the Bishop, he shall lay his hand upon the head of every one severally, saying,

DEFEND, O Lord, this thy Child [or **this thy Servant**] with thy heavenly grace, that **he** may continue thine for ever; and daily increase in thy Holy Spirit, more and more, until **he** come unto thy everlasting kingdom. Amen.

Then shall the Bishop say,
The Lord be with you.

Answer. And with thy spirit.

And (all kneeling down) the Bishop shall add,

Let us pray.

OUR Father which art in heaven, Hallowed be thy Name, Thy kingdom come, Thy will be done, in earth as it is in heaven. Give us this day our daily bread; And forgive us our trespasses, As we forgive them that trespass against us; And lead us not into temptation, But deliver us from evil. Amen.

And this Collect.

ALMIGHTY and everliving God, who makest us both to will and to do those things that be good and acceptable unto thy divine Majesty; We make our humble supplications unto thee for these thy servants, upon whom (after the example of thy holy Apostles) we have now laid our hands, to certify them (by this sign) of thy favour and gracious goodness towards them. Let thy fatherly hand, we beseech thee, ever be over them; let thy Holy Spirit ever be with them; and so lead them in the knowledge and obedience of thy Word, that in the end they may obtain everlasting life; through our Lord Jesus Christ, who with thee and the Holy Ghost liveth and reigneth, ever one God, world without end. **Amen.**

O ALMIGHTY Lord, and everlasting God, vouchsafe, we beseech thee, to direct, sanctify, and govern both our hearts and bodies, in the ways of thy laws, and in the works of thy commandments; that through thy most mighty protection, both here and ever, we may be preserved in body and soul; through our Lord and Saviour Jesus Christ. **Amen.**

Then the Bishop shall bless them, saying thus,

THE blessing of God Almighty, the Father, the Son, and the Holy Ghost, be upon you, and remain with you, for ever. **Amen.**

And there shall none be admitted to the holy Communion, until such time as he be confirmed, or be ready and desirous to be confirmed.

THE FORM
OF SOLEMNIZATION OF
MATRIMONY

First, the Banns of all that are to be married together must be published in the Church three several Sundays, during the time of Morning Service, or of Evening Service, (if there be no Morning Service,) immediately after the second Lesson; the Curate saying after the accustomed manner, **I publish the Banns of Marriage between M. of — and N. of —. If any of you know cause, or just impediment, why these two persons should not be joined together in holy Matrimony, ye are to declare it. This is the first [second, or third] time of asking.**

And if the persons that are to be married dwell in divers Parishes, the Banns must be asked in both Parishes; and the Curate of the one Parish shall not solemnize Matrimony betwixt them, without a Certificate of the Banns being thrice asked, from the Curate of the other Parish.

At the day and time appointed for solemnization of Matrimony, the persons to be married shall come into the Body of the Church with their friends and neighbours: and there standing together, the Man on the right hand, and the Woman on the left, the Priest shall say,

DEARLY beloved, we are gathered together here in the sight of God, and in the face of this Congregation, to join together this man and this woman in holy Matrimony; which is an honourable estate, instituted of God in the time of man's innocency, signifying unto us the mystical union that is betwixt Christ and his Church; which holy estate Christ adorned and beautified with his presence, and first miracle that he wrought, in Cana of Galilee; and is commended of Saint Paul to be honourable among all men: and therefore is not by any to be enterprised, nor taken in hand, unadvisedly, lightly, or wantonly, to satisfy men's carnal lusts and appetites, like brute beasts that have no understanding; but reverently, discreetly, advisedly, soberly, and in the fear of God; duly considering the causes for which Matrimony was ordained.

First, It was ordained for the procreation of children, to be brought up in the fear and nurture of the Lord, and to the praise of his holy Name.

Secondly, It was ordained for a remedy against sin, and to avoid fornication; that such persons as have not the gift of continency might marry, and keep themselves undefiled members of Christ's body.

Thirdly, It was ordained for the mutual society, help, and comfort, that the one ought to have of the other, both in prosperity and adversity. Into which holy estate these two persons present come now to be joined. Therefore if any man can shew any just cause, why they may not lawfully be joined together, let him now speak, or else hereafter for ever hold his peace.

And also, speaking unto the persons that shall be married, he shall say,

I REQUIRE and charge you both, as ye will answer at the dreadful day of judgement, when the secrets of all hearts shall be disclosed, that if either of you know any impediment, why ye may not be lawfully joined together in Matrimony, ye do now confess it. For be ye well assured, that so many as are coupled together otherwise than God's Word doth allow are not joined together by God; neither is their Matrimony lawful.

At which day of Marriage, if any man do allege and declare any impediment, why they may not be coupled together in Matrimony, by God's law, or the laws of this Realm; and will be bound, and sufficient sureties with him, to the parties; or else put in a caution (to the full value of such charges as the persons to be married do thereby sustain) to prove his allegation: then the solemnization must be deferred, until such time as the truth be tried.

If no impediment be alleged, then shall the Curate say unto the Man,

N. WILT thou have this woman to thy wedded wife, to live together after God's ordinance in the holy estate of Matrimony? Wilt thou love her, comfort her, honour, and keep her, in sickness and in health; and, forsaking all other, keep thee only unto her, so long as ye both shall live?

The Man shall answer,
I will.

Then shall the Priest say unto the Woman,

N. WILT thou have this man to thy wedded husband, to live together after God's ordinance in the holy estate of Matrimony? Wilt thou obey him, and serve him, love, honour, and keep him, in sickness and in health; and, forsaking all other, keep thee only unto him, so long as ye both shall live?

The Woman shall answer,

I will.

Then shall the Minister say,

Who giveth this woman to be married to this man?

Then shall they give their troth to each other in this manner.

The Minister, receiving the Woman at her father's or friend's hands, shall cause the Man with his right hand to take the Woman by her right hand, and to say after him as followeth.

I N. take thee **N.** to my wedded wife, to have and to hold from this day forward, for better for worse, for richer for poorer, in sickness and in health, to love and to cherish, till death us do part, according to God's holy ordinance; and thereto I plight thee my troth.

Then shall they loose their hands; and the Woman, with her right hand taking the Man by his right hand, shall likewise say after the Minister,

I **N**. take thee N. to my wedded husband, to have and to hold from this day forward, for better for worse, for richer for poorer, in sickness and in health, to love, cherish, and to obey, till death us do part, according to God's holy ordinance; and thereto I give thee my troth.

Then shall they again loose their hands; and the Man shall give unto the Woman a Ring, laying the same upon the book with the accustomed duty to the Priest and Clerk. And the Priest, taking the Ring, shall deliver it unto the Man, to put it upon the fourth finger of the Woman's left hand. And the Man holding the Ring there, and taught by the Priest, shall say,

WITH this ring I thee wed, with my body I thee worship, and with all my worldly goods I thee endow: In the Name of the Father, and of the Son, and of the Holy Ghost. Amen.

Then the Man leaving the Ring upon the fourth finger of the Woman's left hand, they shall both kneel down, and the Minister shall say,

Let us pray.

O ETERNAL God, Creator and Preserver of all mankind, Giver of all spiritual grace, the Author of everlasting life: Send thy blessing upon these thy servants, this man and this woman, whom we bless in thy Name; that, as Isaac and Rebecca lived faithfully together, so these persons may surely perform and keep the vow and covenant betwixt them made, (whereof this ring given and received is a token and pledge,) and may ever remain in perfect love and peace together, and live according to thy laws; through Jesus Christ our Lord. **Amen.**

Then shall the Priest join their right lands together, and say,

Those whom God hath joined together let no man put asunder.

Then shall the Minister speak unto the people.

FORASMUCH as N. and **N.** have consented

together in holy wedlock, and have witnessed the same before God and this company, and thereto have given and pledged their troth either to other, and have declared the same by giving and receiving of a ring, and by joining of hands; I pronounce that they be man and wife together, In the Name of the Father, and of the Son, and of the Holy Ghost. Amen.

And the Minister shall add this Blessing.

GOD the Father, God the Son, God the Holy Ghost, bless, preserve, and keep you; the Lord mercifully with his favour look upon you, and so fill you with all spiritual benediction and grace, that ye may so live together in this life, that in the world to come ye may have life everlasting. **Amen.**

Then the Minister or Clerks, going to the Lord's Table, shall say or sing this Psalm following.

BEATI OMNES. PSALM 128

BLESSED are all they that fear the Lord : and walk in his ways.

For thou shalt eat the labour of thine hands : O well is thee, and happy shalt thou be.

Thy wife shall be as the fruitful vine : upon the walls of thy house;

Thy children like the olive branches : round about thy table.

Lo, thus shall the man be blessed : that feareth the Lord.

The Lord from out of Sion shall so bless thee : that thou shalt see Jerusalem in prosperity all thy life long;

Yea, that thou shalt see thy children's children : and peace upon Israel.

Glory be to the Father, and to the Son : and to the Holy Ghost;

As it was in the beginning, is now, and ever shall be : world without end. Amen.

Or this Psalm.

DEUS MISEREATUR. PSALM 67

GOD be merciful unto us, and bless us : and shew us the light of his countenance, and be merciful unto us:

That thy way may be known upon earth : thy saving health among all nations.

Let the people praise thee, O God : yea, let all the people praise thee.

O let the nations rejoice and be glad : for thou shalt judge the folk righteously, and govern the nations upon earth.

Let the people praise thee, O God : yea, let all the people praise thee.

Then shall the earth bring forth her increase : and God, even our own God, shall give us his blessing.

God shall bless us : and all the ends of the world shall fear him.

Glory be to the Father, and to the Son : and to the Holy Ghost;

As it was in the beginning, is now, and ever shall be : world without end. Amen.

The Psalm ended, and the Man and the Woman kneeling before the Lord's Table, the Priest standing at the Table, and turning his face towards them, shall say,

Lord, have mercy upon us.

Answer. Christ, have mercy upon us.

Minister. Lord, have mercy upon us.

OUR father which art in heaven, Hallowed be thy Name, Thy kingdom come, Thy will be done, in earth as it is in heaven. Give us this day our daily bread; And forgive us our trespasses, As we forgive them that trespass against us; And lead us not into temptation, But deliver us from evil. Amen.

Minister. O Lord, save thy servant, and thy handmaid;

Answer. Who put their trust in thee.

Minister. O Lord, send them help from thy holy place;

Answer. And evermore defend them.

Minister. Be unto them a tower of strength,

Answer. From the face of their enemy.

Minister. O Lord, hear our prayer;

Answer. And let our cry come unto thee.

Minister.

O GOD of Abraham, God of Isaac, God of Jacob, bless these thy servants, and sow the seed of eternal life in their hearts; that whatsoever in thy holy Word they shall profitably learn, they may in deed fulfil the same. Look, O Lord, mercifully upon them from heaven, and bless them. And as thou didst send thy blessing upon Abraham and Sarah, to their great comfort, so vouchsafe to send thy blessing upon these thy servants; that they obeying thy will, and alway being in safety under thy protection, may abide in thy love unto their lives' end; through Jesus Christ our Lord. **Amen.**

This Prayer next following shall be omitted, where the Woman is past child-bearing.

O MERCIFUL Lord, and heavenly Father, by whose gracious gift mankind is increased: We beseech thee, assist with thy blessing these two persons, that they may both be fruitful in procreation of children, and also live together so long in godly love and honesty, that they may see their children christianly and virtuously brought up, to thy praise and honour; through Jesus Christ our Lord. **Amen.**

O GOD, who by thy mighty power hast made all things of nothing; who also (after other things set in order) didst appoint, that out of man (created after thine own image and similitude) woman should take her beginning; and, knitting them together, didst teach that it should never be lawful to put asunder those whom thou by Matrimony hadst made one: O God, who hast consecrated the state of Matrimony to such an excellent mystery, that in it is signified and represented the spiritual marriage and unity betwixt Christ and his Church: Look mercifully upon these thy servants, that both this man may love his wife, according to thy Word, (as Christ did love his spouse the Church, who gave himself for it, loving and cherishing it even as his own flesh,) and also that this woman may be loving and amiable, faithful and obedient to her husband; and in all quietness, sobriety, and peace, be a follower of holy and godly matrons. O Lord, bless them both, and grant them to inherit thy everlasting kingdom; through Jesus Christ our Lord. **Amen.**

Then shall the Priest say,

ALMIGHTY God, who at the beginning did create our first parents, Adam and Eve, and did sanctify and join them together in marriage; Pour upon you the riches of his grace, sanctify and bless you, that ye may please him both in body and soul, and live together in holy love unto your lives' end. **Amen.**

After which, if there be no Sermon declaring the duties of Man and Wife, the Minister shall read as followeth.

ALL ye that are married, or that intend to take the holy estate of Matrimony upon you, hear what the holy Scripture doth say as touching the duty of husbands towards their wives, and wives towards their husbands.

Saint Paul, in his Epistle to the Ephesians, the fifth Chapter, doth give this commandment to all married men; Husbands, love your wives, even as Christ also loved the Church, and gave himself for it, that he might sanctify and cleanse it with the washing of water, by the word; that he might present it to himself a glorious Church, not having spot, or wrinkle, or any such thing; but that it should be holy, and without blemish. So ought men to love their wives as their own bodies. He that loveth his wife loveth himself: for no man ever yet hated his own flesh, but nourisheth and cherisheth it, even as the Lord the Church: for we are members of his body, of his flesh, and of his bones. For this cause shall a man leave his father and mother, and shall be joined unto his wife; and they two shall be one flesh. This is a great mystery; but I speak concerning Christ and the Church. Nevertheless, let every one of you in particular so love his wife, even as himself.

Likewise the same Saint Paul, writing to the Colossians, speaketh thus to all men that are married; Husbands, love your wives, and be not bitter against them.

Hear also what Saint Peter, the Apostle of Christ, who was himself a married man, saith unto them that are married; Ye husbands, dwell with your wives according to knowledge;

giving honour unto the wife, as unto the weaker vessel, and as being heirs together of the grace of life, that your prayers be not hindered.

Hitherto ye have heard the duty of the husband toward the wife. Now likewise, ye wives, hear and learn your duties toward your husbands, even as it is plainly set forth in holy Scripture.

Saint Paul, in the aforenamed Epistle to the Ephesians, teacheth you thus; Wives, submit yourselves unto your own husbands, as unto the Lord. For the husband is the head of the wife, even as Christ is the head of the Church: and he is the Saviour of the body. Therefore as the Church is subject unto Christ, so let the wives be to their own husbands in every thing. And again he saith, Let the wife see that she reverence her husband.

And in his Epistle to the Colossians, Saint Paul giveth you this short lesson; Wives, submit yourselves unto your own husbands, as it is fit in the Lord.

Saint Peter also doth instruct you very well, thus saying; Ye wives, be in subjection to your own husbands; that, if any obey not the word, they also may without the word be won by the conversation of the wives; while they behold your chaste conversation coupled with fear. Whose adorning, let it not be that outward adorning of plaiting the hair, and of wearing of gold, or of putting on of apparel; but let it be the hidden man of the heart, in that which is not corruptible; even the ornament of a meek and quiet spirit, which is in the sight of God of great price. For after this manner in the old time the holy women also, who trusted in God, adorned themselves, being in subjection unto their own husbands; even as Sarah obeyed Abraham, calling him lord; whose daughters ye are as long as ye do well, and are not afraid with any amazement.

It is convenient that the new-married persons should receive the holy Communion at the time of their Marriage, or at the first opportunity after their Marriage.

THE ORDER FOR
THE VISITATION
OF THE SICK

When any person is sick, notice shall be given thereof to the Minister of the Parish; who, coming into the sick person's house, shall say,

PEACE be to this house, and to all that dwell in it.

When he cometh into the sick man's presence he shall say, kneeling down,

REMEMBER not, Lord, our iniquities, nor the iniquities of our forefathers: Spare us, good Lord, spare thy people, whom thou hast redeemed with thy most precious blood, and be not angry with us for ever.

Answer. Spare us, good Lord.

Then the Minister shall say,
Let us pray.

Lord, have mercy upon us.
Christ, have mercy upon us.
Lord, have mercy upon us.

OUR Father which art in heaven, Hallowed be thy Name, Thy kingdom come, Thy will be done, in earth as it is in heaven. Give us this day our daily bread; And forgive us our trespasses, As we forgive them that trespass against us; And lead us not into temptation, But deliver us from evil. Amen.

Minister. O Lord, save thy servant;

Answer. Which putteth **his** trust in thee.

Minister. Send **him** help from thy holy place;

Answer. And evermore mightily defend **him**.

Minister. Let the enemy have no advantage of him;

Answer. Nor the wicked approach to hurt him.

Minister. Be unto **him**, O Lord, a strong tower,

Answer. From the face of **his** enemy.

Minister. O Lord, hear our prayers;

Answer. And let our cry come unto thee.

Minister.

O LORD, look down from heaven, behold, visit, and relieve this thy servant. Look upon him with the eyes of thy mercy, give him comfort and sure confidence in thee, defend him from the danger of the enemy, and keep him in perpetual peace and safety; through Jesus Christ our Lord. **Amen.**

HEAR us, Almighty and most merciful God and Saviour; extend thy accustomed goodness to this thy servant who is grieved with sickness. Sanctify, we beseech thee, this thy fatherly correction to **him**; that the sense of **his** weakness may add strength to **his** faith, and seriousness to **his** repentance: that, if it shall be thy good pleasure to restore **him** to **his** former health, **he** may lead the residue of **his** life in thy fear, and to thy glory: or else give **him** grace so to take thy visitation, that, after this painful life ended, **he** may dwell with thee in life everlasting; through Jesus Christ our Lord. **Amen.**

Then shall the Minister exhort the sick person after this form, or other like.

DEARLY beloved, know this, that Almighty God is the Lord of life and death, and of all things to them pertaining, as youth, strength, health, age, weakness, and sickness. Wherefore, whatsoever your sickness is, know you certainly, that it is God's visitation. And for what cause soever this sickness is sent unto you; whether it be to try your patience, for the example of others, and that your faith may be found in the day of the Lord laudable, glorious, and honourable, to the increase of glory and endless felicity; or else it be sent unto you to correct and amend in you whatsoever doth offend the eyes of your heavenly Father; know you certainly, that if you truly repent you of your sins, and bear your sickness patiently, trusting in God's mercy for his dear Son Jesus Christ's sake, and render unto him humble thanks for his fatherly visitation, submitting yourself wholly unto his will, it shall turn to your profit, and help you forward in the right way that leadeth unto everlasting life.

If the person visited be very sick, then the Curate may end his exhortation in this place, or else proceed.

TAKE therefore in good part the chastisement of the Lord: For (as Saint Paul saith in the twelfth chapter to the Hebrews) whom the Lord loveth he chasteneth, and scourgeth every son whom he receiveth. If ye endure chastening, God dealeth with you as with sons; for what son is he whom the father chasteneth not? But if ye be without chastisement, whereof all are partakers, then are ye bastards, and not sons. Furthermore, we have had fathers of our flesh, which corrected us, and we gave them reverence: shall we not much rather be in subjection unto the Father of spirits, and live? For they verily for a few days chastened us after their own pleasure; but he for our profit, that we might be partakers of his holiness. These words, good **brother**, are written in holy Scripture for our comfort and instruction, that we should patiently, and with thanksgiving, bear our heavenly Father's correction, whensoever by any manner of adversity it shall please his gracious goodness to visit us. And there should be no greater comfort to Christian persons, than to be made like unto Christ, by suffering patiently adversities, troubles, and sicknesses. For he himself went not up to joy, but first he suffered pain; he entered not into his glory before he was crucified. So truly our way to eternal joy is to suffer here with Christ; and our door to enter into eternal life is gladly to die with Christ; that we may rise again from death, and dwell with him in everlasting life. Now therefore, taking your sickness, which is thus profitable for you, patiently, I exhort you, in the name of God, to remember the profession which you made unto God in your Baptism. And forasmuch as after this life there is an account to be given unto the righteous Judge, by whom all must be judged without respect of persons, I require you to examine yourself and your estate, both toward God and man; so that, accusing and condemning yourself for your own faults, you may find mercy at our heavenly Father's hand for Christ's sake, and not be accused and condemned in that fearful judgement. Therefore I shall rehearse to you the Articles of our Faith, that you may know whether you do believe as a Christian man should, or no.

Here the Minister shall rehearse the Articles of the Faith, saying thus,

DOST thou believe in God the Father Almighty, Maker of heaven and earth?

And in Jesus Christ his only-begotten Son our Lord? And that he was conceived by the Holy Ghost, born of the Virgin Mary; that he suffered under Pontius Pilate, was crucified, dead, and buried; that he went down into hell, and also did rise again the third day; that he ascended into heaven, and sitteth at the right hand of God the Father Almighty; and from thence shall come again at the end of the world, to judge the quick and the dead?

And dost thou believe in the Holy Ghost; the holy Catholick Church; the Communion of Saints; the Remission of sins; the Resurrection of the flesh; and everlasting life after death?

The sick person shall answer,
All this I stedfastly believe.

Then shall the Minister examine whether he repent him truly of his sins, and be in charity with all the world; exhorting him to forgive, from the bottom of his heart, all persons that have offended him; and if he have offended any other, to ask them forgiveness; and where he hath done injury or wrong to any man, that he make amends to the uttermost of his power. And if he have not before disposed of his goods, let him then be admonished to make his Will, and to declare his debts, what he oweth, and what is owing unto him; for the better discharging of his conscience, and the quietness of his Executors. But men should often be put in remembrance to take order for the settling of their temporal estates whilst they are in health.

These words before rehearsed may be said before the Minister begin his Prayer, as he shall see cause.

The Minister should not omit earnestly to move such sick persons as are of ability to be liberal to the poor.

Here shall the sick person be moved to make a special confession of his sins, if he feel his conscience troubled with any weighty matter. After which confession, the Priest shall absolve him (if he humbly and heartily desire it) after this sort.

OUR Lord Jesus Christ, who hath left power to his Church to absolve all sinners who truly repent and believe in him, of his great mercy forgive thee thine offences: And by his authority committed to me, I absolve thee from all thy sins, In the Name of the Father, and of the Son, and of the Holy Ghost. Amen.

And then the Priest shall say the Collect following.

Let us pray.

O MOST merciful God, who, according to the multitude of thy mercies, dost so put away the sins of those who truly repent, that thou rememberest them no more: Open thine eye of mercy upon this thy servant, who most earnestly desireth pardon and forgiveness. Renew in **him** (most loving Father) whatsoever hath been decayed by the fraud and malice of the devil, or by **his** own carnal will and frailness; preserve and continue this sick member in the unity of the Church; consider **his** contrition, accept **his** tears, asswage **his** pain, as shall seem to thee most expedient for **him**. And forasmuch as **he** putteth **his** full trust only in thy mercy, impute not unto **him his** former sins, but strengthen **him** with thy blessed Spirit; and, when thou art pleased to take **him** hence, take **him** unto thy favour, through the merits of thy most dearly beloved Son Jesus Christ our Lord. **Amen.**

Then shall the Minister say this Psalm.

IN TE, DOMINE, SPERAVI. PSALM 71

IN thee, O Lord, have I put my trust; let me never be put to confusion : but rid me, and deliver me in thy righteousness; incline thine ear unto me, and save me.

Be thou my strong hold, whereunto I may alway resort : thou hast promised to help me; for thou art my house of defence, and my castle.

Deliver me, O my God, out of the hand of the ungodly : out of the hand of the unrighteous and cruel man.

For thou, O Lord God, art the thing that I long for : thou art my hope, even from my youth.

Through thee have I been holden up ever

since I was born : thou art he that took me out of my mother's womb; my praise shall alway be of thee.

I am become as it were a monster unto many: but my sure trust is in thee.

O let my mouth be filled with thy praise : that I may sing of thy glory and honour all the day long.

Cast me not away in the time of age : forsake me not when my strength faileth me.

For mine enemies speak against me, and they that lay wait for my soul take their counsel together, saying : God hath forsaken him, persecute him, and take him; for there is none to deliver him.

Go not far from me, O God : my God, haste thee to help me.

Let them be confounded and perish that are against my soul : let them be covered with shame and dishonour that seek to do me evil.

As for me, I will patiently abide alway : and will praise thee more and more.

My mouth shall daily speak of thy righteousness and salvation : for I know no end thereof.

I will go forth in the strength of the Lord God: and will make mention of thy righteousness only.

Thou, O God, hast taught me from my youth up until now : therefore will I tell of thy wondrous works.

Forsake me not, O God, in mine old age, when I am gray-headed : until I have shewed thy strength unto this generation, and thy power to all them that are yet for to come.

Thy righteousness, O God, is very high, and great things are they that thou hast done : O God, who is like unto thee?

Glory be to the Father, and to the Son : and to the Holy Ghost;

As it was in the beginning, is now, and ever shall be : world without end. Amen.

Adding this.

O SAVIOUR of the world, who by thy Cross and precious Blood hast redeemed us: Save us, and help us, we humbly beseech thee, O Lord.

Then shall the Minister say,

THE Almighty Lord, who is a most strong tower to all them that put their trust in him, to whom all things in heaven, in earth, and under the earth, do bow and obey, be now and evermore thy defence; and make thee know and feel, that there is none other Name under heaven given to man, in whom, and through whom, thou mayest receive health and salvation, but only the Name of our Lord Jesus Christ. Amen.

And after that shall say,

UNTO God's gracious mercy and protection we commit thee. The Lord bless thee, and keep thee. The Lord make his face to shine upon thee, and be gracious unto thee. The Lord lift up his countenance upon thee, and give thee peace, both now and evermore. **Amen.**

A PRAYER FOR A SICK CHILD.

O ALMIGHTY God, and merciful Father, to whom alone belong the issues of life and death: Look down from heaven, we humbly beseech thee, with the eyes of mercy upon this child now lying upon the bed of sickness. Visit **him**, O Lord, with thy salvation; deliver **him** in thy good appointed time from **his** bodily pain, and save **his** soul for thy mercies' sake: that, if it shall be thy pleasure to prolong **his** days here on earth, **he** may live to thee, and be an instrument of thy glory, by serving thee faithfully, and doing good in **his** generation; or else receive **him** into those heavenly habitations, where the souls of them that sleep in the Lord Jesus enjoy perpetual rest and felicity. Grant this, O Lord, for thy mercies' sake, in the same thy Son our Lord Jesus Christ, who liveth and reigneth with thee and the Holy Ghost, ever one God, world without end. **Amen.**

A PRAYER FOR A SICK PERSON, WHEN THERE APPEARETH SMALL HOPE OF RECOVERY.

O FATHER of mercies, and God of all comfort, our only help in time of need: We fly unto thee for succour in behalf of this thy servant, here lying under thy hand in great weakness of body. Look graciously upon **him**, O Lord; and the more the outward man decayeth, strengthen **him**, we beseech thee, so much the more continually with thy grace and Holy Spirit in the inner man. Give **him** unfeigned repentance for all the errors of **his** life past, and stedfast faith in thy Son Jesus; that **his** sins may be done away by thy mercy, and **his** pardon sealed in heaven, before **he** go hence, and be no more seen. We know, O Lord, that there is no word impossible with thee; and that, if thou wilt, thou canst even yet raise **him** up, and grant **him** a longer continuance amongst us: Yet, forasmuch as in all appearance the time of **his** dissolution draweth near, so fit and prepare him, we beseech thee, against the hour of death, that after **his** departure hence in peace, and in thy favour, **his** soul may be received into thine everlasting kingdom, through the merits and mediation of Jesus Christ, thine only Son, our Lord and Saviour. **Amen.**

A COMMENDATORY PRAYER FOR A SICK PERSON AT THE POINT OF DEPARTURE.

O ALMIGHTY God, with whom do live the spirits of just men made perfect, after they are delivered from their earthly prisons: We humbly commend the soul of this thy servant, our dear **brother**, into thy hands, as into the hands of a faithful Creator, and most merciful Saviour; most humbly beseeching thee that it may be precious in thy sight. Wash it, we pray thee, in the blood of that immaculate Lamb, that was slain to take away the sins of the world; that whatsoever defilements it may have contracted in the midst of this miserable and naughty world, through the lusts of the flesh or the wiles of Satan, being purged and done away, it may be presented pure and without spot before thee. And teach us who survive, in this and other like daily spectacles of mortality, to see how frail and uncertain our own condition is; and so to number our days, that we may seriously apply our hearts to that holy and heavenly wisdom, whilst we live here,

which may in the end bring us to life everlasting, through the merits of Jesus Christ, thine
only Son our Lord. **Amen.**

A PRAYER FOR PERSONS TROUBLED IN MIND OR IN CONSCIENCE.

O BLESSED Lord, the Father of mercies, and the
God of all comforts: We beseech thee, look
down in pity and compassion upon this thy
afflicted servant. Thou writest bitter things
against **him**, and makest **him** to possess **his**
former iniquities; thy wrath lieth hard upon
him, and **his** soul is full of trouble: But, O
merciful God, who hast written thy holy Word
for our learning, that we, through patience and
comfort of thy holy Scriptures, might have
hope; give **him** a right understanding of
himself, and of thy threats and promises; that
he may neither cast away his confidence in
thee, nor place it any where but in thee. Give
him strength against all **his** temptations, and
heal all **his** distempers. Break not the bruised
reed, nor quench the smoking flax. Shut not

up thy tender mercies in displeasure; but make **him** to hear of joy and gladness, that the bones which thou hast broken may rejoice. Deliver **him** from fear of the enemy, and lift up the light of thy countenance upon **him**, and give **him** peace, through the merits and mediation of Jesus Christ our Lord. **Amen.**

THE
COMMUNION OF THE SICK

Forasmuch as all mortal men be subject to many sudden perils, diseases and sicknesses, and ever uncertain what time they shall depart out of this life; therefore, to the intent they may be always in a readiness to die, whensoever it shall please Almighty God to call them, the Curates shall diligently from time to time (but especially in the time of pestilence, or other infectious sickness) exhort their Parishioners to the often receiving of the holy Communion of the Body and Blood of our Saviour Christ, when it shall be publickly administered in the Church; that so doing, they may, in case of sudden visitation, have the less cause to be disquieted for lack of the same. But if the sick person be not able to come to the Church, and yet is desirous to receive the Communion in his house; then he must give timely notice to the Curate, signifying also how many there are to communicate with him, (which shall be three, or two at the least,) and having a convenient place in the sick man's house, with all things necessary so prepared, that the Curate may reverently minister, he shall there celebrate the holy Communion, beginning with the Collect, Epistle, and Gospel here following.

THE COLLECT

ALMIGHTY everliving God, Maker of mankind, who dost correct those whom thou dost love, and chastise every one whom thou dost receive: We beseech thee to have mercy upon this thy servant visited with thine hand; and to grant that he may take his sickness patiently, and recover his bodily health, (if it be thy gracious will,) and whensoever his soul shall depart from the body, it may be without spot presented unto thee; through Jesus Christ our Lord. **Amen.**

THE EPISTLE. Hebr. 12. 5

MY son, despise not thou the chastening of the Lord, nor faint when thou art rebuked of him. For whom the Lord loveth he chasteneth, and scourgeth every son whom he receiveth.

THE GOSPEL. S. John 5. 24

VERILY, verily I say unto you, He that heareth my word, and believeth on him that sent me, hath everlasting life, and shall not come into condemnation; but is passed from death unto life.

After which the Priest shall proceed according to the form before prescribed for the holy Communion, beginning at these words [**Ye that do truly, &c.**], p. 95.

At the time of the distribution of the holy Sacrament, the Priest shall first receive the Communion himself, and after minister unto them that are appointed to communicate with the sick; and last of all to the sick person.

But if a man, either by reason of extremity of sickness, or for want of warning in due time to the Curate, or for lack of company to receive with him, or by any other just impediment, do not receive the Sacrament of Christ's Body and Blood: the Curate shall instruct him that if he do truly repent him of his sins, and stedfastly believe that Jesus Christ hath suffered death upon the Cross for him, and shed his Blood for his redemption, earnestly remembering the benefits he hath thereby, and giving him hearty thanks therefore; he doth eat and drink the Body and Blood of our Saviour Christ profitably to his soul's health, although he do not receive the Sacrament with his mouth.

When the sick person is visited and receiveth the holy Communion all at one time, then the Priest, for more expedition, shall cut off the form of the Visitation at the Psalm [**In thee, O Lord, have I put my trust**] and go straight to the Communion.

In the time of the plague, sweat, or such other like contagious times of sickness or diseases, when none of the Parish or neighbours can be gotten to communicate with the sick in their houses, for fear of the infection, upon special request of the diseased, the Minister may only communicate with him.

THE ORDER FOR
THE BURIAL OF
THE DEAD

The Priest and Clerks meeting the corpse at the entrance of the Church-yard, and going before it, either into the Church, or towards the grave, shall say, or sing:

I AM the resurrection and the life, saith the Lord: he that believeth in me, though he were dead, yet shall he live: and whosoever liveth and believeth in me shall never die.

S. John 11. 25, 26.

I KNOW that my Redeemer liveth, and that he shall stand at the latter day upon the earth. And though after my skin worms destroy this body, yet in my flesh shall I see God: whom I shall see for myself, and mine eyes shall behold, and not another.   *Job* 19. 25, 26, 27.

WE brought nothing into this world, and it is certain we can carry nothing out. The Lord gave, and the Lord hath taken away; blessed be the name of the Lord.   1 *Tim.* 6. 7. *Job* 1. 21.

After they are come into the Church, shall be read one or both of these Psalms following.

DIXI, CUSTODIAM. PSALM 39

I SAID, I will take heed to my ways : that I offend not in my tongue.

I will keep my mouth as it were with a bridle : while the ungodly is in my sight.

I held my tongue, and spake nothing : I kept silence, yea, even from good words; but it was pain and grief to me.

My heart was hot within me, and while I was thus musing the fire kindled : and at the last I spake with my tongue;

Lord, let me know mine end, and the number of my days : that I may be certified how long I have to live.

Behold, thou hast made my days as it were a span long : and mine age is even as nothing in respect of thee; and verily every man living is altogether vanity.

For man walketh in a vain shadow, and disquieteth himself in vain : he heapeth up riches, and cannot tell who shall gather them.

And now, Lord, what is my hope : truly my hope is even in thee.

Deliver me from all mine offences : and make me not a rebuke unto the foolish.

I became dumb, and opened not my mouth: for it was thy doing.

Take thy plague away from me : I am even consumed by means of thy heavy hand.

When thou with rebukes dost chasten man for sin, thou makest his beauty to consume away, like as it were a moth fretting a garment : every man therefore is but vanity.

Hear my prayer, O Lord, and with thine ears consider my calling : hold not thy peace at my tears.

For I am a stranger with thee : and a sojourner, as all my fathers were.

O spare me a little, that I may recover my

strength : before I go hence, and be no more seen.

Glory be to the Father, and to the Son : and to the Holy Ghost;

As it was in the beginning, is now, and ever shall be : world without end. Amen.

DOMINE, REFUGIUM. PSALM 90

LORD, thou hast been our refuge : from one generation to another.

Before the mountains were brought forth, or ever the earth and the world were made : thou art God from everlasting, and world without end.

Thou turnest man to destruction: again thou sayest, Come again, ye children of men.

For a thousand years in thy sight are but as yesterday : seeing that is past as a watch in the night.

As soon as thou scatterest them, they are even as a sleep : and fade away suddenly like the grass.

In the morning it is green, and groweth up:

but in the evening it is cut down, dried up, and withered.

For we consume away in thy displeasure : and are afraid at thy wrathful indignation.

Thou hast set our misdeeds before thee : and our secret sins in the light of thy countenance.

For when thou art angry, all our days are gone: we bring our years to an end, as it were a tale that is told.

The days of our age are threescore years and ten; and though men be so strong, that they come to fourscore years : yet is their strength then but labour and sorrow; so soon passeth it away, and we are gone.

But who regardeth the power of thy wrath : for even thereafter as a man feareth, so is thy displeasure.

O teach us to number our days : that we may apply our hearts unto wisdom.

Turn thee again, O Lord, at the last : and be gracious unto thy servants.

O satisfy us with thy mercy, and that soon :

so shall we rejoice and be glad all the days of our life.

Comfort us again now after the time that thou hast plagued us : and for the years wherein we have suffered adversity.

Shew thy servants thy work : and their children thy glory.

And the glorious majesty of the Lord our God be upon us : prosper thou the work of our hands upon us, O prosper thou our handywork.

Glory be to the Father, and to the Son : and to the Holy Ghost;

As it was in the beginning, is now, and ever shall be : world without end. Amen.

Then shall follow the Lesson taken out of the fifteenth chapter of the former Epistle of Saint Paul to the Corinthians.

1 COR. 15. 20

NOW is Christ risen from the dead, and become the first-fruits of them that slept. For since by man came death, by man came also the resurrection of the dead. For as in Adam all die, even so in Christ shall all be made alive. But every man in his own order: Christ the first-fruits; afterward they that are Christ's, at his coming. Then cometh the end, when he shall have delivered up the kingdom to God, even the Father; when he shall have put down all rule, and all authority, and power. For he must reign, till he hath put all enemies under his feet. The last enemy that shall be destroyed is death. For he hath put all things under his feet. But when he saith, all things are put under him, it is manifest that he is excepted, which did put all things under him. And when all things shall be subdued unto him, then shall the Son also himself be subject unto him that put all things under him, that God may be all in all. Else what shall they do which are baptized for the dead, if the dead rise not at all? why are they then baptized for the dead? And why stand we in jeopardy every hour? I protest by your rejoicing, which I have in Christ Jesus our Lord, I die daily. If after the manner of men I have fought with beasts at Ephesus, what advantageth it me, if the dead rise not? Let us eat and drink, for to-morrow we die. Be not deceived: evil communications corrupt good manners. Awake to righteousness, and sin not: for some have not the knowledge of God: I speak this to your shame. But some man will say, How are the dead raised up? and with what body do they come? Thou fool, that which thou sowest is not quickened, except it die. And that which thou sowest, thou sowest not that body that shall be, but bare grain, it may chance of wheat, or of some other grain: but God giveth it a body, as it hath pleased him, and to every seed his own body. All flesh is not the same flesh; but there is one kind of flesh of men, another flesh of beasts, another of fishes, and another of birds. There are also celestial bodies, and bodies terrestrial; but the glory of the celestial is one, and the glory of the terrestrial is another. There is one glory of the sun, and another glory of the moon, and another glory of the stars; for one star differeth from another star in glory. So also is the resurrection of the dead. It is sown in corruption; it is raised in incorruption: it is sown in dishonour; it is raised in glory: it is sown in weakness; it is raised in power: it is sown a natural body; it is raised a spiritual body. There is a natural body, and there is a spiritual body. And so it is written, The first man Adam was made a living soul; the last Adam was made a quickening spirit. Howbeit, that was not first which is spiritual, but that which is natural; and afterward that which is spiritual. The first man is of the earth, earthy: the second man is the Lord from heaven. As is the earthy, such are they that are earthy: and as is the heavenly, such are they also that are heavenly. And as we have borne the image of the earthy, we shall also bear the image of the heavenly. Now this I say, brethren, that flesh and blood cannot inherit the kingdom of God; neither doth corruption inherit incorruption. Behold, I shew you a mystery: We shall not all sleep, but we shall all be changed, in a moment, in the twinkling of an eye, at the last trump: for the trumpet shall sound, and the dead shall be raised incorruptible, and we shall be changed. For this corruptible must put on incorruption, and this mortal must put on immortality. So when this corruptible shall have put on incorruption, and this mortal shall have put on immortality; then shall be brought to pass the saying that is written, Death is swallowed up in victory. O death, where is thy sting? O grave, where is thy victory? The sting of death is sin; and the strength of sin is the law. But thanks be to God, which giveth us the victory through our Lord Jesus Christ. Therefore, my beloved brethren, be ye stedfast, unmoveable, always abounding in the work of the Lord, forasmuch as ye know that your labour is not in vain in the Lord.

When they come to the grave, while the corpse is made ready to be laid into the earth, the Priest shall say, or the Priest and Clerks shall sing:

MAN that is born of a woman hath but a short time to live, and is full of misery. He cometh up, and is cut down, like a flower; he fleeth as it were a shadow, and never continueth in one stay.

In the midst of life we are in death: of whom may we seek for succour, but of thee, O Lord, who for our sins art justly displeased?

Yet, O Lord God most holy, O Lord most mighty, O holy and most merciful Saviour, deliver us not into the bitter pains of eternal death.

Thou knowest, Lord, the secrets of our hearts; shut not thy merciful ears to our prayer; but spare us, Lord most holy, O God most mighty, O holy and merciful Saviour, thou most worthy Judge eternal, suffer us not, at our last hour, for any pains of death, to fall from thee.

Then, while the earth shall be cast upon the body by some standing by, the Priest shall say,

FORASMUCH as it hath pleased Almighty God of his great mercy to take unto himself the soul of our dear brother here departed: we therefore commit his body to the ground;

earth to earth, ashes to ashes, dust to dust; in sure and certain hope of the Resurrection to eternal life, through our Lord Jesus Christ; who shall change our vile body, that it may be like unto his glorious body, according to the mighty working, whereby he is able to subdue all things to himself.

Then shall be said or sung,

I HEARD a voice from heaven, saying unto me, Write, From henceforth blessed are the dead which die in the Lord: Even so, saith the Spirit, for they rest from their labours.

Then the Priest shall say,

Lord, have mercy upon us.
Christ, have mercy upon us.
Lord, have mercy upon us.

OUR Father which art in heaven, Hallowed be thy Name, Thy kingdom come, Thy will be done, in earth as it is in heaven. Give us this day our daily bread; And forgive us our trespasses, As we forgive them that trespass against us; And lead us not into temptation, But deliver us from evil. Amen.

Priest.

ALMIGHTY God, with whom do live the spirits of them that depart hence in the Lord, and with whom the souls of the faithful, after they are delivered from the burden of the flesh, are in joy and felicity: We give thee hearty thanks, for that it hath pleased thee to deliver this our brother out of the miseries of this sinful world; beseeching thee that it may please thee, of thy gracious goodness, shortly to accomplish the number of thine elect, and to hasten thy kingdom; that we, with all those that are departed in the true faith of thy holy Name, may have our perfect consummation and bliss, both in body and soul, in thy eternal and everlasting glory; through Jesus Christ our Lord. **Amen.**

THE COLLECT

O MERCIFUL God, the Father of our Lord Jesus Christ, who is the resurrection and the life; in whom whosoever believeth shall live, though he die; and whosoever liveth, and believeth in him, shall not die eternally; who also hath taught us (by his holy Apostle Saint Paul) not to be sorry, as men without hope, for them that sleep in him: We meekly beseech thee, O Father, to raise us from the death of sin unto the life of righteousness; that, when we shall depart this life, we may rest in him, as our hope is this our brother doth; and that, at the general Resurrection in the last day, we may be found acceptable in thy sight, and receive that blessing, which thy well-beloved Son shall then pronounce to all that love and fear thee, saying, Come, ye blessed children of my Father, receive the kingdom prepared for you from the beginning of the world: Grant this, we beseech thee, O merciful Father, through Jesus Christ, our Mediator and Redeemer. **Amen.**

THE grace of our Lord Jesus Christ, and the love of God, and the fellowship of the Holy Ghost, be with us all evermore. **Amen.**

THE THANKSGIVING OF WOMEN AFTER CHILD-BIRTH
COMMONLY CALLED
THE CHURCHING OF WOMEN

The Woman, at the usual time after her delivery, shall come into the Church decently apparelled, and there shall kneel down in some convenient place, as hath been accustomed, or as the Ordinary shall direct: And then the Priest shall say unto her,

FORASMUCH as it hath pleased Almighty God of his goodness to give you safe deliverance, and hath preserved you in the great danger of child-birth: You shall therefore give hearty thanks unto God, and say,

Then shall the Priest say the 116th Psalm.

DILEXI QUONIAM

I AM well pleased : that the Lord hath heard the voice of my prayer;

That he hath inclined his ear unto me : therefore will I call upon him as long as I live.

The snares of death compassed me round about: and the pains of hell gat hold upon me.

I found trouble and heaviness, and I called upon the name of the Lord : O Lord, I beseech thee, deliver my soul.

Gracious is the Lord, and righteous: yea, our God is merciful.

The Lord preserveth the simple : I was in misery, and he helped me.

Turn again then unto thy rest, O my soul : for the Lord hath rewarded thee.

And why? thou hast delivered my soul from death : mine eyes from tears, and my feet from falling.

I will walk before the Lord : in the land of the living.

I believed, and therefore will I speak; but I was sore troubled : I said in my haste, All men are liars.

What reward shall I give unto the Lord : for all the benefits that he hath done unto me?

I will receive the cup of salvation : and call upon the name of the Lord.

I will pay my vows now in the presence of all his people : in the courts of the Lord's house, even in the midst of thee, O Jerusalem. Praise the Lord.

Glory be to the Father, and to the Son : and to the Holy Ghost;

As it was in the beginning, is now, and ever shall be : world without end. Amen.

Or Psalm 127.

NISI DOMINUS

EXCEPT the Lord build the house : their labour is but lost that build it.

Except the Lord keep the city : the watchman waketh but in vain.

It is but lost labour that ye haste to rise up early, and so late take rest, and eat the bread of carefulness : for so he giveth his beloved sleep.

Lo, children and the fruit of the womb : are an heritage and gift that cometh of the Lord.

Like as the arrows in the hand of the giant: even so are the young children.

Happy is the man that hath his quiver full of

them : they shall not be ashamed when they speak with their enemies in the gate.

Glory be to the Father, and to the Son : and to the Holy Ghost;

As it was in the beginning, is now, and ever shall be : world without end. Amen.

Then the Priest shall say,

Let us pray.

Lord, have mercy upon us.
Christ, have mercy upon us.
Lord, have mercy upon us.

OUR Father which art in heaven, Hallowed be thy Name, Thy kingdom come, Thy will be done, in earth as it is in heaven. Give us this day our daily bread; And forgive us our trespasses, As we forgive them that trespass against us; And lead us not into temptation, But deliver us from evil. For thine is the kingdom, the power, and the glory, For ever and ever. Amen.

Minister. O Lord, save this woman thy servant;

Answer. Who putteth her trust in thee.
Minister. Be thou to her a strong tower;
Answer. From the face of her enemy.
Minister. Lord, hear our prayer.
Answer. And let our cry come unto thee.

Minister.

Let us pray.

O ALMIGHTY God, we give thee humble thanks for that thou hast vouchsafed to deliver this woman thy servant from the great pain and peril of child-birth: Grant, we beseech thee, most merciful Father, that she through thy help may both faithfully live and walk according to thy will, in this life present; and also may be partaker of everlasting glory in the life to come; through Jesus Christ our Lord. **Amen.**

The Woman, that cometh to give her thanks, must offer accustomed offerings; and, if there be a Communion, it is convenient that she receive the holy Communion.

A COMMINATION

OR DENOUNCING OF GOD'S ANGER AND JUDGEMENTS AGAINST SINNERS

WITH CERTAIN PRAYERS TO BE USED ON THE FIRST DAY OF LENT, AND AT OTHER TIMES, AS THE ORDINARY SHALL APPOINT

After Morning Prayer, the Litany ended, according to the accustomed manner, the Priest shall in the reading Pew or Pulpit say,

BRETHREN, in the primitive Church there was a godly discipline, that, at the beginning of Lent, such persons as stood convicted of notorious sin were put to open penance, and punished in this world, that their souls might be saved in the day of the Lord; and that others, admonished by their example, might be the more afraid to offend.

Instead whereof, until the said discipline may be restored again, (which is much to be wished,) it is thought good that at this time (in the presence of you all) should be read the general sentences of God's cursing against impenitent sinners, gathered out of the seven and twentieth chapter of Deuteronomy, and other places of Scripture; and that ye should answer to every sentence, **Amen**: To the intent that, being admonished of the great indignation of God against sinners, ye may the rather be moved to earnest and true repentance; and may walk more warily in these dangerous days; fleeing from such vices, for which ye affirm with your own mouths the curse of God to be due.

CURSED is the man that maketh any carved or molten image, to worship it.

And the people shall answer and say,
Amen.

Minister. Cursed is he that curseth his father or mother.

Answer. Amen.

Minister. Cursed is he that removeth his neighbour's land-mark.

Answer. Amen.

Minister. Cursed is he that maketh the blind to go out of his way.

Answer. Amen.

Minister. Cursed is he that perverteth the judgement of the stranger, the fatherless, and widow.

Answer. Amen.

Minister. Cursed is he that smiteth his neighbour secretly.

Answer. Amen.

Minister. Cursed is he that lieth with his neighbour's wife.

Answer. Amen.

Minister. Cursed is he that taketh reward to slay the innocent.

Answer. Amen.

Minister. Cursed is he that putteth his trust in man, and taketh man for his defence, and in his heart goeth from the Lord.

Answer. Amen.

Minister. Cursed are the unmerciful, fornicators, and adulterers, covetous persons, idolaters, slanderers, drunkards, and extortioners.

Answer. Amen.

Minister.

NOW seeing that all they are accursed (as the prophet David beareth witness) who do err and go astray from the commandments of God; let us (remembering the dreadful judgement hanging over our heads, and always ready to fall upon us) return unto our Lord God with all contrition and meekness of heart; bewailing and lamenting our sinful life, acknowledging and confessing our offences, and seeking to bring forth worthy fruits of penance. For now is the axe put unto the root of the trees, so that every tree that bringeth not forth good fruit is hewn down, and cast into the fire. It is a fearful thing to fall into the hands of the living God: He shall pour down rain upon the sinners, snares, fire and brimstone, storm and tempest; this shall be their portion to drink. For lo, the Lord is come out of his place to visit the wickedness of such as dwell upon the earth. But who may abide the day of his coming? Who shall be able to endure when he appeareth? His fan is in his hand, and he will purge his floor, and gather his wheat into the barn; but he will burn the chaff with unquenchable fire. The day of the Lord cometh as a thief in the night: and when men shall say, Peace, and all things are safe, then shall sudden destruction come upon them, as sorrow cometh upon a woman travailing with child, and they shall not escape. Then shall appear the wrath of God in the day of vengeance, which obstinate sinners, through the stubbornness of their heart, have heaped unto themselves; which despised the good-ness, patience, and long-sufferance of God, when he calleth them continually to repen-tance. Then shall they call upon me (saith the Lord) but I will not hear; they shall seek me early, but they shall not find me; and that, because they hated knowledge, and received not the fear of the Lord, but abhorred my counsel, and despised my correction. Then shall it be too late to knock, when the door shall be shut; and too late to cry for mercy, when it is the time of justice. O terrible voice of most just judgement, which shall be pronounced upon them, when it shall be said unto them, Go, ye cursed, into the fire everlasting, which is prepared for the devil and his angels. Therefore, brethren, take we heed betime, while the day of salvation lasteth; for the night cometh, when none can work: But let us, while we have the light, believe in the light, and walk as children of the light; that we be not cast into utter darkness, where is weeping and gnashing of teeth. Let us not abuse the goodness of God, who calleth us mercifully to amendment, and of his endless pity promiseth us forgiveness of that which is past, if with a perfect and true heart we return unto him. For though our sins be as red as scarlet, they shall be made white as snow; and though they be like purple, yet they shall be made white as wool. Turn ye (saith the Lord) from all your wickedness, and your sin shall not be your destruction: Cast away from you all your ungodliness that ye have done: Make you new hearts, and a new spirit: Wherefore will ye die,

O ye house of Israel? seeing that I have no pleasure in the death of him that dieth, saith the Lord God. Turn ye then, and ye shall live. Although we have sinned, yet have we an Advocate with the Father, Jesus Christ the righteous; and he is the propitiation for our sins. For he was wounded for our offences, and smitten for our wickedness. Let us therefore return unto him, who is the merciful receiver of all true penitent sinners; assuring ourselves that he is ready to receive us, and most willing to pardon us, if we come unto him with faithful repentance; if we submit ourselves unto him, and from henceforth walk in his ways; if we will take his easy yoke and light burden upon us, to follow him in lowliness, patience, and charity, and be ordered by the governance of his Holy Spirit; seeking always his glory, and serving him duly in our vocation with thanksgiving. This if we do, Christ will deliver us from the curse of the law, and from the extreme male-diction which shall light upon them that shall be set on the left hand; and he will set us on his right hand, and give us the gracious benediction of his Father, commanding us to take possession of his glorious kingdom: Unto which he vouchsafe to bring us all, for his infinite mercy. Amen.

Then shall they all kneel upon their knees, and the Priest and Clerks kneeling (in the place where they are accustomed to say the Litany) shall say this Psalm.

MISERERE MEI, DEUS. PSALM 51

HAVE mercy upon me, O God, after thy great goodness : according to the multitude of thy mercies do away mine offences.

Wash me throughly from my wickedness : and cleanse me from my sin.

For I acknowledge my faults : and my sin is ever before me.

Against thee only have I sinned, and done this evil in thy sight : that thou mightest be justified in thy saying, and clear when thou art judged.

Behold, I was shapen in wickedness : and in sin hath my mother conceived me.

But lo, thou requirest truth in the inward

parts : and shalt make me to understand wisdom secretly.

Thou shalt purge me with hyssop, and I shall be clean : thou shalt wash me, and I shall be whiter than snow.

Thou shalt make me hear of joy and gladness : that the bones which thou hast broken may rejoice.

Turn thy face away from my sins : and put out all my misdeeds.

Make me a clean heart, O God : and renew a right spirit within me.

Cast me not away from thy presence : and take not thy holy Spirit from me.

O give me the comfort of thy help again : and stablish me with thy free Spirit.

Then shall I teach thy ways unto the wicked: and sinners shall be converted unto thee.

Deliver me from blood-guiltiness, O God, thou that art the God of my health : and my tongue shall sing of thy righteousness.

Thou shalt open my lips, O Lord : and my mouth shall shew thy praise.

For thou desirest no sacrifice, else would I give it thee : but thou delightest not in burnt-offering.

The sacrifice of God is a troubled spirit : a broken and contrite heart, O God, shalt thou not despise.

O be favourable and gracious unto Sion : build thou the walls of Jerusalem.

Then shalt thou be pleased with the sacrifice of righteousness, with the burnt-offerings and oblations : then shall they offer young bullocks upon thine altar.

Glory be to the Father, and to the Son : and to the Holy Ghost;

Answer. As it was in the beginning, is now, and ever shall be : world without end. Amen.

Lord, have mercy upon us.
Christ, have mercy upon us.
Lord, have mercy upon us.

OUR Father which art in heaven, Hallowed be thy Name, Thy kingdom come, Thy will be done, in earth as it is in heaven. Give us this day our daily bread; And forgive us our trespasses, As we forgive them that trespass against us; And lead us not into temptation, But deliver us from evil. Amen.

Minister. O Lord, save thy servants;

Answer. That put their trust in thee.

Minister. Send unto them help from above.

Answer. And evermore mightily defend them.

Minister. Help us, O God our Saviour.

Answer. And for the glory of thy Name deliver us; be merciful unto us sinners, for thy Name's sake.

Minister. O Lord, hear our prayer.

Answer. And let our cry come unto thee.

Minister.
Let us pray.

O LORD, we beseech thee, mercifully hear our prayers, and spare all those who confess their sins unto thee; that they, whose consciences by sin are accused, by thy merciful pardon may be absolved; through Christ our Lord. **Amen.**

O MOST mighty God, and merciful Father, who hast compassion upon all men, and hatest nothing that thou hast made; who wouldest not the death of a sinner, but that he should rather turn from his sin, and be saved: Mercifully forgive us our trespasses; receive and comfort us, who are grieved and wearied with the burden of our sins. Thy property is always to have mercy; to thee only it appertaineth to forgive sins. Spare us therefore, good Lord, spare thy people, whom thou hast redeemed; enter not into judgement with thy servants, who are vile earth, and miserable sinners; but so turn thine anger from us, who meekly acknowledge our vileness, and truly repent us of our faults, and so make haste to help us in this world, that we may ever live with thee in the world to come; through Jesus Christ our Lord. **Amen.**

Then shall the people say this that followeth, after the Minister.

TURN thou us, O good Lord, and so shall we be turned. Be favourable, O Lord, Be favourable to thy people, Who turn to thee in weeping, fasting, and praying. For thou art a merciful God, Full of compassion, long-suffering, and of great pity. Thou sparest when we deserve punishment, And in thy wrath thinkest upon mercy. Spare thy people, good Lord, Spare them, and let not thine heritage be brought to confusion. Hear us, O Lord, for thy mercy is great, And after the multitude of thy mercies look upon us; Through the merits and mediation of thy blessed Son, Jesus Christ our Lord. Amen.

Then the Minister alone shall say,

THE Lord bless us, and keep us; the Lord lift up the light of his countenance upon us, and give us peace, now and for evermore. **Amen.**

FORMS OF PRAYER
TO BE
USED AT SEA

The Morning and Evening Service to be used daily at Sea shall be the same which is appointed in the Book of Common Prayer.

These two following Prayers are to be also used in her Majesty's Navy every day.

O ETERNAL Lord God, who alone spreadest out the heavens, and rulest the raging of the sea; who hast compassed the waters with bounds until day and night come to an end: Be pleased to receive into thy Almighty and most gracious protection the persons of us thy servants, and the Fleet in which we serve. Preserve us from the dangers of the sea, and from the violence of the enemy; that we may be a safeguard unto our most gracious Sovereign Lady, Queen **ELIZABETH,** and her Dominions, and a security for such as pass on the seas upon their lawful occasions; that the inhabitants of our Island may in peace and quietness serve thee our

God; and that we may return in safety to enjoy the blessings of the land, with the fruits of our labours; and with a thankful remembrance of thy mercies to praise and glorify thy holy Name; through Jesus Christ our Lord. **Amen.**

THE COLLECT

PREVENT us, O Lord, in all our doings, with thy most gracious favour, and further us with thy continual help; that in all our works begun, continued, and ended in thee, we may glorify thy holy Name, and finally by thy mercy obtain everlasting life; through Jesus Christ our Lord. **Amen.**

PRAYERS TO BE USED IN STORMS AT SEA.

O MOST powerful and glorious Lord God, at whose command the winds blow, and lift up the waves of the sea, and who stillest the rage thereof: We thy creatures, but miserable sinners, do in this our great distress cry unto thee for help: Save, Lord, or else we perish. We confess, when we have been safe, and seen all things quiet about us, we have forgot thee our God, and refused to hearken to the still voice of thy word, and to obey thy commandments: But now we see how terrible thou art in all thy works of wonder; the great God to be feared above all: And therefore we adore thy Divine Majesty, acknowledging thy power, and imploring thy goodness. Help, Lord, and save us for thy mercy's sake in Jesus Christ thy Son, our Lord. **Amen.**

Or this:

O MOST glorious and gracious Lord God, who dwellest in heaven, but beholdest all things below: Look down, we beseech thee, and hear us, calling out of the depth of misery, and out of the jaws of this death, which is ready now to swallow us up: Save, Lord, or else we perish. The living, the living shall praise thee. O send thy word of command to rebuke the raging winds, and the roaring sea; that we, being delivered from this distress, may live to serve thee, and to glorify thy Name all the days of our life. Hear, Lord, and save us, for the infinite merits of our blessed Saviour, thy Son, our Lord Jesus Christ. **Amen.**

THE PRAYER TO BE SAID BEFORE A FIGHT AT SEA AGAINST ANY ENEMY.

O MOST powerful and glorious Lord God, the Lord of hosts, that rulest and commandest all things: Thou sittest in the throne judging right, and therefore we make our address to thy Divine Majesty in this our necessity, that thou wouldest take the cause into thine own hand, and judge between us and our enemies. Stir up thy strength, O Lord, and come and help us; for thou givest not alway the battle to the strong, but canst save by many or by few. O let not our sins now cry against us for vengeance; but hear us thy poor servants begging mercy, and imploring thy help, and that thou wouldest be a defence unto us against the face of the enemy. Make it appear that thou art our Saviour and mighty Deliverer; through Jesus Christ our Lord. **Amen.**

GENERAL PRAYERS.

Short Prayers for single persons that cannot meet to join in Prayer with others, by reason of the Fight, or Storm.

LORD, be merciful to us sinners, and save us for thy mercy's sake.

Thou art the great God, that hast made and rulest all things: O deliver us for thy Name's sake.

Thou art the great God to be feared above all: O save us, that we may praise thee.

SPECIAL PRAYERS WITH RESPECT TO THE ENEMY.

THOU, O Lord, art just and powerful: O defend our cause against the face of the enemy.

O God, thou art a strong tower of defence to all that flee unto thee: O save us from the violence of the enemy.

O Lord of hosts, fight for us, that we may glorify thee.

O suffer us not to sink under the weight of our sins, or the violence of the enemy.

O Lord, arise, help us, and deliver us for thy Name's sake.

SHORT PRAYERS IN RESPECT OF A STORM.

THOU, O Lord, that stillest the raging of the sea: hear, hear us, and save us, that we perish not.

O blessed Saviour, that didst save thy disciples ready to perish in a storm: hear us, and save us, we beseech thee.

Lord, have mercy upon us.
Christ, have mercy upon us.
Lord, have mercy upon us.
O Lord, hear us.
O Christ, hear us.

God the Father, God the Son, God the Holy Ghost, have mercy upon us, save us now and evermore. Amen.

OUR Father which art in heaven, Hallowed be thy Name, Thy kingdom come, Thy will be done, in earth as it is in heaven. Give us this day our daily bread; And forgive us our trespasses, As we forgive them that trespass against us; And lead us not into temptation, But deliver us from evil. For thine is the kingdom, the power, and the glory, For ever and ever. Amen.

When there shall be imminent danger, as many as can be spared from necessary service in the Ship shall be called together, and make an humble Confession of their sin to God: In which every one ought seriously to reflect upon those particular sins of which his conscience shall accuse him: saying as followeth.

THE CONFESSION

ALMIGHTY God, Father of our Lord Jesus Christ, Maker of all things, Judge of all men: We acknowledge and bewail our manifold sins and wickedness, Which we from time to time most grievously have committed, By thought, word, and deed, Against thy Divine Majesty, Provoking most justly thy wrath and indignation against us. We do earnestly repent, And are heartily sorry for these our misdoings; The remembrance of them is grievous unto us; The burden of them is intolerable. Have mercy upon us, Have mercy upon us, most merciful Father; For thy Son our Lord Jesus Christ's sake, Forgive us all that is past; And grant that we may ever hereafter Serve and please thee In newness of life, To the honour and glory of thy Name; Through Jesus Christ our Lord. Amen.

Then shall the Priest, if there be any in the Ship, pronounce this Absolution.

ALMIGHTY God, our heavenly Father, who of his great mercy hath promised forgiveness of sins to all them that with hearty repentance and true faith turn unto him; Have mercy upon you; pardon and deliver you from all your sins; confirm and strengthen you in all goodness; and bring you to everlasting life; through Jesus Christ our Lord. **Amen.**

THANKSGIVING AFTER A STORM.

JUBILATE DEO. PSALM 66

O BE joyful in God, all ye lands : sing praises unto the honour of his Name, make his praise to be glorious.

Say unto God, O how wonderful art thou in thy works : through the greatness of thy power shall thine enemies be found liars unto thee.

For all the world shall worship thee : sing of thee, and praise thy Name.

O come hither, and behold the works of God : how wonderful he is in his doing toward the children of men.

He turned the sea into dry land : so that they went through the water on foot; there did we rejoice thereof.

He ruleth with his power for ever; his eyes behold the people : and such as will not believe shall not be able to exalt themselves.

O praise our God, ye people : and make the voice of his praise to be heard;

Who holdeth our soul in life: and suffereth not our feet to slip.

For thou, O God, hast proved us : thou also hast tried us, like as silver is tried.

Thou broughtest us into the snare : and laidest trouble upon our loins.

Thou sufferedst men to ride over our heads : we went through fire and water, and thou broughtest us out into a wealthy place.

I will go into thine house with burnt-offerings: and will pay thee my vows, which I promised with my lips, and spake with my mouth, when I was in trouble.

I will offer unto thee fat burnt-sacrifices, with the incense of rams : I will offer bullocks and goats.

O come hither, and hearken, all ye that fear God: and I will tell you what he hath done for my soul.

I called unto him with my mouth : and gave him praises with my tongue.

If I incline unto wickedness with mine heart : the Lord will not hear me.

But God hath heard me : and considered the voice of my prayer.

Praised be God, who hath not cast out my prayer : nor turned his mercy from me.

Glory be to the Father, and to the Son: and to the Holy Ghost;

As it was in the beginning, is now, and ever shall be : world without end. Amen.

CONFITEMINI DOMINO. PSALM 107

O GIVE thanks unto the Lord, for he is gracious : and his mercy endureth for ever.

Let them give thanks whom the Lord hath redeemed : and delivered from the hand of the enemy;

And gathered them out of the lands, from the east and from the west : from the north and from the south.

They went astray in the wilderness out of the way : and found no city to dwell in;

Hungry and thirsty : their soul fainted in them.

So they cried unto the Lord in their trouble : and he delivered them from their distress.

He led them forth by the right way : that they might go to the city where they dwelt.

O that men would therefore praise the Lord for his goodness : and declare the wonders that he doeth for the children of men!

For he satisfieth the empty soul : and filleth the hungry soul with goodness.

Such as sit in darkness, and in the shadow of death : being fast bound in misery and iron;

Because they rebelled against the words of the Lord : and lightly regarded the counsel of the most Highest;

He also brought down their heart through heaviness : they fell down, and there was none to help them up.

So when they cried unto the Lord in their trouble : he delivered them out of their distress.

For he brought them out of darkness, and out of the shadow of death : and brake their bonds in sunder.

O that men would therefore praise the Lord for his goodness : and declare the wonders that he doeth for the children of men! For he hath broken the gates of brass: and smitten the bars of iron in sunder.

Foolish men are plagued for their offence : and because of their wickedness.

Their soul abhorred all manner of meat : and they were even hard at death's door.

So when they cried unto the Lord in their trouble : he delivered them out of their distress.

He sent his word, and healed them : and they were saved from their destruction.

O that men would therefore praise the Lord for his goodness : and declare the wonders that he doeth for the children of men!

That they would offer unto him the sacrifice of thanksgiving : and tell out his works with gladness!

They that go down to the sea in ships : and occupy their business in great waters;

These men see the works of the Lord : and his wonders in the deep.

For at his word the stormy wind ariseth : which lifteth up the waves thereof.

They are carried up to the heaven, and down again to the deep : their soul melteth away because of the trouble.

They reel to and fro, and stagger like a drunken man : and are at their wits' end.

So when they cry unto the Lord in their trouble : he delivereth them out of their distress.

For he maketh the storm to cease : so that the waves thereof are still.

Then are they glad, because they are at rest : and so he bringeth them unto the haven where they would be.

O that men would therefore praise the Lord for his goodness : and declare the wonders that he doeth for the children of men!

That they would exalt him also in the congregation of the people : and praise him in the seat of the elders!

Who turneth the floods into a wilderness : and drieth up the water-springs.

A fruitful land maketh he barren : for the wickedness of them that dwell therein.

Again, he maketh the wilderness a standing water : and water-springs of a dry ground.

And there he setteth the hungry : that they may build them a city to dwell in;

That they may sow their land, and plant vineyards : to yield them fruits of increase.

He blesseth them, so that they multiply exceedingly : and suffereth not their cattle to decrease.

And again, when they are minished and brought low : through oppression, through any plague or trouble;

Though he suffer them to be evil intreated through tyrants : and let them wander out of the way in the wilderness;

Yet helpeth he the poor out of misery : and maketh him households like a flock of sheep.

The righteous will consider this, and rejoice : and the mouth of all wickedness shall be stopped.

Whoso is wise will ponder these things : and they shall understand the loving-kindness of the Lord.

Glory be to the Father, and to the Son : and to the Holy Ghost;

As it was in the beginning, is now, and ever shall be : world without end. Amen.

COLLECTS OF THANKSGIVING.

O MOST blessed and glorious Lord God, who art of infinite goodness and mercy: We thy poor creatures, whom thou hast made and preserved, holding our souls in life, and now rescuing us out of the jaws of death, humbly present ourselves again before thy Divine Majesty, to offer a sacrifice of praise and thanksgiving, for that thou heardest us when we called in our trouble, and didst not cast out our prayer, which we made before thee in our great distress: Even when we gave all for lost, our ship, our goods, our lives, then didst thou mercifully look upon us, and wonderfully command a deliverance; for which we, now being in safety, do give all praise and glory to thy holy Name; through Jesus Christ our Lord. **Amen.**

Or this:

O MOST mighty and gracious good God, thy mercy is over all thy works, but in special manner hath been extended toward us, whom thou hast so powerfully and wonderfully defended. Thou hast shewed us terrible things, and wonders in the deep, that we might see how powerful and gracious a God thou art; how able and ready to help them that trust in thee. Thou hast shewed us how both winds and seas obey thy command; that we may learn, even from them, hereafter to obey thy voice, and to do thy will. We therefore bless and glorify thy Name, for this thy mercy in saving us, when we were ready to perish. And, we beseech thee, make us as truly sensible now of thy mercy, as we were then of the danger: and give us hearts always ready to express our thankfulness, not only by words, but also by our lives, in being more obedient to thy holy commandments. Continue, we beseech thee, this thy goodness to us; that we, whom thou hast saved, may serve thee in holiness and righteousness all the days of our life; through Jesus Christ our Lord and Saviour. **Amen.**

A HYMN OF PRAISE AND THANKSGIVING
AFTER A DANGEROUS TEMPEST.

O COME, let us give thanks unto the Lord, for he is gracious : and his mercy endureth for ever.

Great is the Lord, and greatly to be praised; let the redeemed of the Lord say so : whom he hath delivered from the merciless rage of the sea.

The Lord is gracious and full of compassion: slow to anger, and of great mercy.

He hath not dealt with us according to our sins : neither rewarded us according to our iniquities.

But as the heaven is high above the earth : so great hath been his mercy towards us.

We found trouble and heaviness : we were even at death's door.

The waters of the sea had well-nigh covered us : the proud waters had well-nigh gone over our soul.

The sea roared : and the stormy wind lifted up the waves thereof.

We were carried up as it were to heaven, and then down again into the deep : our soul melted within us, because of trouble;

Then cried we unto thee, O Lord : and thou didst deliver us out of our distress.

Blessed be thy Name, who didst not despise the prayer of thy servants : but didst hear our cry, and hast saved us.

Thou didst send forth thy commandment : and the windy storm ceased, and was turned into a calm.

O let us therefore praise the Lord for his goodness : and declare the wonders that he hath done, and still doeth, for the children of men.

Praised be the Lord daily : even the Lord that helpeth us, and poureth his benefits upon us.

He is our God, even the God of whom cometh salvation : God is the Lord by whom we have escaped death.

Thou, Lord, hast made us glad through the operation of thy hands : and we will triumph in thy praise.

Blessed be the Lord God : even the Lord God, who only doeth wondrous things;

And blessed be the Name of his majesty for ever : and let every one of us say, Amen, Amen.

Glory be to the Father, and to the Son : and to the Holy Ghost;

As it was in the beginning, is now, and ever shall be : world without end. Amen.

2 CORINTHIANS 13.

THE grace of our Lord Jesus Christ, and the love of God, and the fellowship of the Holy Ghost, be with us all evermore. **Amen.**

AFTER VICTORY OR DELIVERANCE FROM AN ENEMY.

A Psalm or Hymn of Praise and Thanksgiving after Victory.

IF the Lord had not been on our side, now may we say : if the Lord himself had not been on our side, when men rose up against us;

They had swallowed us up quick : when they were so wrathfully displeased at us.

Yea, the waters had drowned us, and the stream had gone over our soul : the deep waters of the proud had gone over our soul.

But praised be the Lord : who hath not given us over as a prey unto them.

The Lord hath wrought : a mighty salvation for us.

We gat not this by our own sword, neither was it our own arm that saved us : but thy right hand, and thine arm, and the light of thy countenance, because thou hadst a favour unto us.

The Lord hath appeared for us : the Lord hath covered our heads, and made us to stand in the day of battle.

The Lord hath appeared for us : the Lord hath overthrown our enemies, and dashed in pieces those that rose up against us.

Therefore not unto us, O Lord, not unto us : but unto thy Name be given the glory.

The Lord hath done great things for us : the Lord hath done great things for us, for which we rejoice.

Our help standeth in the Name of the Lord : who hath made heaven and earth.

Blessed be the Name of the Lord : from this time forth for evermore.

Glory be to the Father, and to the Son : and to the Holy Ghost;

As it was in the beginning, is now, and ever shall be : world without end. Amen.

After this Hymn may be sung the TE DEUM.

Then this Collect.

O ALMIGHTY God, the Sovereign Commander of all the world, in whose hand is power and might which none is able to withstand: We bless and magnify thy great and glorious Name for this happy Victory, the whole glory whereof we do ascribe to thee, who art the only giver of Victory. And, we beseech thee, give us grace to improve this great mercy to thy glory, the advancement of thy Gospel, the honour of our Sovereign, and, as much as in us lieth, to the good of all mankind. And, we beseech thee, give us such a sense of this great mercy, as may engage us to a true thankfulness, such as may appear in our lives by an humble, holy, and obedient walking before thee all our days, through Jesus Christ our Lord; to whom with thee and the Holy Spirit, as for all thy mercies, so in particular for this Victory and Deliverance, be all glory and honour, world without end. **Amen.**

2 CORINTHIANS 13.

THE grace of our Lord Jesus Christ, and the love of God, and the fellowship of the Holy Ghost, be with us all evermore. **Amen**.

AT THE BURIAL OF THEIR DEAD AT SEA

The Office in the Common-Prayer-Book may be used: only instead of these words [We therefore commit his body to the ground, earth to earth, &c.] say,

WE therefore commit his body to the deep, to be turned into corruption, looking for the resurrection of the body, (when the Sea shall give up her dead,) and the life of the world to come, through our Lord Jesus Christ; who at his coming shall change our vile body, that it may be like his glorious body, according to the mighty working, whereby he is able to subdue all things to himself.

FORMS OF PRAYER

WITH THANKSGIVING TO ALMIGHTY GOD

For use in all Churches and Chapels within this Realm, every Year, upon the Anniversary of the day of the Accession of the Reigning Sovereign, or upon such other day as shall be appointed by Authority.

I

At Mattins and Evensong the following Psalms, Lessons, Suffrages, and Collects may be used.

Proper Psalms, 20, 101, 121.

Proper Lessons.

The First, Joshua 1 to verse 10, **or** Proverbs 8 to verse 17.

The Second, Rom. 13 to verse 11, **or** Rev. 21. 22–22. 4.

The Suffrages next after the Creed.

Priest.

O LORD, shew thy mercy upon us.
    Answer. And grant us thy salvation.
    Priest. O Lord, save the Queen;
    Answer. Who putteth her trust in thee.

Priest. Send her help from thy holy place.

Answer. And evermore mightily defend her.

Priest. Be unto her, O Lord, a strong tower;

Answer. From the face of her enemies.

Priest. Endue thy Ministers with righteousness.

Answer. And make thy chosen people joyful.

Priest. O Lord, save thy people.

Answer. And bless thine inheritance.

Priest. Give peace in our time, O Lord.

Answer. Because there is none other that fighteth for us, but only thou, O God.

Priest. O Lord, hear our prayer;

Answer. And let our cry come unto thee.

After the first Collect, at Morning or Evening Prayer, the following Collect.

O GOD, who providest for thy people by thy power, and rulest over them in love: Vouchsafe so to bless thy Servant our Queen, that under her this nation may be wisely governed, and thy Church may serve thee in all godly quietness; and grant that she being devoted to thee with her whole heart, and persevering in good works unto the end, may, by thy guidance, come to thine everlasting kingdom; through Jesus Christ thy Son our Lord, who liveth and reigneth with thee and the Holy Ghost, ever one God, world without end. **Amen.**

If the Litany be sung or said, these Prayers immediately after the Prayer, We humbly beseech thee: and if the Litany be not said, then these Prayers instead of the Prayers for the Queen and for the Royal Family at Mattins or Evensong.

O LORD our God, who upholdest and governest all things by the word of thy power: Receive our humble prayers for our Sovereign Lady **ELIZABETH, as on this day,** set over us by thy grace and providence to be our Queen; and, together with her, bless, we beseech thee, **Philip** Duke of Edinburgh, **Charles** Prince of Wales, and all the Royal Family; that they, ever trusting in thy goodness, protected by thy power, and crowned with thy gracious and endless favour, may long continue before thee in peace and safety, joy and honour, and after death may obtain everlasting life and glory, by the merits and mediation of Christ Jesus our Saviour, who with thee and the Holy Ghost liveth and reigneth ever one God, world without end. **Amen.**

ALMIGHTY God, who rulest over all the kingdoms of the world, and dost order them according to thy good pleasure: We yield thee unfeigned thanks, for that thou wast pleased, **as on this day**, to set thy Servant our Sovereign Lady, Queen **ELIZABETH**, upon the Throne of this Realm. Let thy wisdom be her guide, and let thine arm strengthen her; let truth and justice, holiness and righteousness, peace and charity, abound in her days; direct all her counsels and endeavours to thy glory, and the welfare of her subjects; give us grace to obey her cheerfully for conscience sake, and let her always possess the hearts of her people; let her reign be long and prosperous, and crown her with everlasting life in the world to come; through Jesus Christ our Lord. **Amen.**

A PRAYER FOR UNITY.

O GOD the Father of our Lord Jesus Christ, our only Saviour, the Prince of Peace: Give us grace seriously to lay to heart the great dangers we are in by our unhappy divisions. Take away all hatred and prejudice, and whatsoever else may hinder us from godly union and concord: that, as there is but one Body, and one Spirit, and one hope of our calling, one Lord, one faith, one baptism, one God and Father of us all; so we may henceforth be all of one heart, and of one soul, united in one holy bond of truth and peace, of faith and charity, and may with one mind and one mouth glorify thee; through Jesus Christ our Lord. **Amen.**

II

THE COMMUNION

In the Order of the Administration of Holy Communion, in place of the Collect, Epistle, and Gospel of the day, shall be said the following.

THE COLLECT

O GOD, who providest for thy people by thy power, and rulest over them in love: Vouchsafe so to bless thy Servant our Queen, that under her this nation may be wisely governed, and thy Church may serve thee in all godly quietness; and grant that she being devoted to thee with her whole heart, and persevering in good works unto the end, may, by thy guidance, come to thine everlasting kingdom; through Jesus Christ thy Son our Lord, who liveth and reigneth with thee and the Holy Ghost, ever one God, world without end. **Amen.**

THE EPISTLE. 1 S. Peter 2. 11

DEARLY beloved, I beseech you as strangers and pilgrims, abstain from fleshly lusts, which war against the soul; having your conversation honest among the Gentiles; that, whereas they speak against you as evil-doers, they may, by your good works which they shall behold, glorify God in the day of visitation. Submit yourselves to every ordinance of man for the

Lord's sake; whether it be to the king, as supreme; or unto governors, as unto them that are sent by him, for the punishment of evildoers, and for the praise of them that do well. For so is the will of God, that with well-doing ye may put to silence the ignorance of foolish men: as free, and not using your liberty for a cloke of maliciousness; but as the servants of God. Honour all men. Love the brotherhood. Fear God. Honour the king.

THE GOSPEL. S. Matth. 22. 16

AND they sent out unto him their disciples, with the Herodians, saying, Master, we know that thou art true, and teachest the way of God in truth, neither carest thou for any man: for thou regardest not the person of men. Tell us therefore, What thinkest thou? Is it lawful to give tribute unto Cæsar, or not? But Jesus perceived their wickedness, and said, Why tempt ye me, ye hypocrites? shew me the tribute-money. And they brought unto him a penny. And he saith unto them, Whose is this image and superscription? They say unto him, Cæsar's. Then saith he unto them, Render therefore unto Cæsar the things which are Cæsar's; and unto God the things that are God's. When they had heard these words, they marvelled, and left him, and went their way.

If this day should fall on a Sunday or other Holy-day, the Collect, Epistle, and Gospel of the day shall be used, and the Collect, O God, who providest, shall be said after the Collect of the day.

III

The following Service may also be used on the same day at any convenient time.

TE DEUM LAUDAMUS

WE praise thee, O God : we acknowledge thee to be the Lord.

All the earth doth worship thee : the Father everlasting.

To thee all Angels cry aloud : the heavens and all the powers therein.

To thee Cherubin and Seraphin : continually do cry,

Holy, Holy, Holy : Lord God of Sabaoth;

Heaven and earth are full of the Majesty : of thy glory.

The glorious company of the Apostles : praise thee.

The goodly fellowship of the Prophets : praise thee.

The noble army of Martyrs : praise thee.

The holy Church throughout all the world : doth acknowledge thee;

The Father : of an infinite Majesty;

Thine honourable, true : and only Son;

Also the Holy Ghost : the Comforter.

THOU art the King of glory : O Christ.

Thou art the everlasting Son : of the Father.

When thou tookest upon thee to deliver man : thou didst not abhor the Virgin's womb.

When thou hadst overcome the sharpness of death : thou didst open the kingdom of heaven to all believers.

Thou sittest at the right hand of God : in the glory of the Father.

We believe that thou shalt come : to be our Judge.

We therefore pray thee, help thy servants : whom thou hast redeemed with thy precious blood.

Make them to be numbered with thy Saints : in glory everlasting.

O LORD, save thy people : and bless thine heritage.

Govern them : and lift them up for ever.

Day by day : we magnify thee;

And we worship thy Name : ever world without end.

Vouchsafe, O Lord : to keep us this day without sin.

O Lord, have mercy upon us : have mercy upon us.

O Lord, let thy mercy lighten upon us : as our trust is in thee.

O Lord, in thee have I trusted : let me never be confounded.

Then the Priest shall say,

The Lord be with you.

Answer. And with thy spirit.

Let us pray.

Lord, have mercy upon us.
Christ, have mercy upon us.
Lord, have mercy upon us.

OUR Father which art in heaven, Hallowed be thy Name, Thy kingdom come, Thy will be done, in earth as it is in heaven. Give us this day our daily bread; And forgive us our trespasses, As we forgive them that trespass against us; And lead us not into temptation, But deliver us from evil. Amen.

Then the Priest standing up shall say,

O Lord, save the Queen;
Answer. Who putteth her trust in thee.
Priest. Send her help from thy holy place.
Answer. And evermore mightily defend her.
Priest. Let her enemies have no advantage of her.

Answer. Nor the wicked approach to hurt her.

Priest. O Lord, hear our prayer;

Answer. And let our cry come unto thee.

Let us pray.

O GOD, who providest for thy people by thy power, and rulest over them in love: Vouchsafe so to bless thy Servant our Queen, that under her this nation may be wisely governed, and thy Church may serve thee in all godly quietness; and grant that she being devoted to thee with her whole heart, and persevering in good works unto the end, may, by thy guidance, come to thine everlasting kingdom; through Jesus Christ thy Son our Lord, who liveth and reigneth with thee and the Holy Ghost, ever one God, world without end. **Amen.**

O LORD our God, who upholdest and governest all things by the word of thy power: Receive our humble prayers for our Sovereign Lady **ELIZABETH, as on this day,** set over us by thy grace and providence to be our Queen; and, together with her, bless, we beseech thee, **Philip** Duke of Edinburgh, **Charles** Prince of Wales, and all the Royal Family; that they, ever trusting in thy goodness, protected by thy power, and crowned with thy gracious and endless favour, may long continue before thee in peace and safety, joy and honour, and after death may obtain everlasting life and glory, by the merits and mediation of Christ Jesus our Saviour, who with thee and the Holy Ghost liveth and reigneth ever one God, world without end. **Amen.**

ALMIGHTY God, who rulest over all the kingdoms of the world, and dost order them according to thy good pleasure: We yield thee unfeigned thanks, for that thou wast pleased, **as on this day**, to set thy Servant our Sovereign Lady, Queen **ELIZABETH**, upon the Throne of this Realm. Let thy wisdom be her guide, and let thine arm strengthen her; let truth and justice, holiness and righteousness, peace and charity, abound in her days; direct all her counsels and endeavours to thy glory, and the welfare of her subjects; give us grace to obey her cheerfully for conscience sake, and let her always possess the hearts of her people; let her reign be long and prosperous, and crown her with everlasting life in the world to come; through Jesus Christ our Lord. **Amen.**

A PRAYER FOR UNITY.

O GOD the Father of our Lord Jesus Christ, our only Saviour, the Prince of Peace: Give us grace seriously to lay to heart the great dangers we are in by our unhappy divisions. Take away all hatred and prejudice, and whatsoever else may hinder us from godly union and concord: that, as there is but one Body, and one Spirit, and one hope of our calling, one Lord, one faith, one baptism, one God and Father of us all; so we may henceforth be all of one heart, and of one soul, united in one holy bond of truth and peace, of faith and charity, and may with one mind and one mouth glorify thee; through Jesus Christ our Lord. **Amen.**

ALMIGHTY God, the fountain of all wisdom, who knowest our necessities before we ask, and our ignorance in asking: We beseech thee to have compassion upon our infirmities; and those things, which for our unworthiness we dare not, and for our blindness we cannot ask, vouchsafe to give us for the worthiness of thy Son Jesus Christ our Lord. **Amen.**

THE blessing of God Almighty, the Father, the Son, and the Holy Ghost, be amongst you and remain with you always. **Amen.**

"ELIZABETH R.

"WHEREAS by Our Royal Warrant dated the Twelfth day of June, One thousand nine hundred and fifty-three, certain Forms of Prayer and Service were made for the Sixth day of February and commanded to be printed and published and annexed to the Book of Common Prayer and Liturgy of the Church of England to be used yearly in all Churches and Chapels within the Provinces of Canterbury and York:

"NOW Our Will and Pleasure is that Our said Royal Warrant be revoked, and that the use of the said Forms of Prayer and Service be discontinued; and that the Forms of Prayer and Service hereunto annexed be forthwith printed and published and annexed to the Book of Common Prayer and Liturgy of the Church of England to be used yearly on the Sixth day of February in all Churches and Chapels within the Provinces of Canterbury and York.

"GIVEN at Our Court at Saint James's the Twenty-sixth day of July, 1958; In the Seventh Year of Our Reign.

"By Her Majesty's Command.
R. A. BUTLER."

ARTICLES

AGREED UPON BY THE ARCHBISHOPS
AND BISHOPS OF BOTH PROVINCES AND
THE WHOLE CLERGY IN THE
CONVOCATION HOLDEN AT LONDON IN
THE YEAR 1562 FOR THE AVOIDING OF
DIVERSITIES OF OPINIONS AND FOR
THE ESTABLISHING OF CONSENT
TOUCHING TRUE RELIGION

REPRINTED
BY COMMAND OF HIS MAJESTY
KING CHARLES I
WITH HIS ROYAL DECLARATION
PREFIXED THEREUNTO

CPSIA information can be obtained
at www.ICGtesting.com
Printed in the USA
LVHW061916080421
683893LV00006BA/410

9 781108 498616